ON THE EDGE OF
THE MYSTERY

GORDON S. WAKEFIELD

ON THE EDGE OF
THE MYSTERY

*Meditations on Passages from
the Communion Service*

LONDON
EPWORTH PRESS

© GORDON S. WAKEFIELD 1969

First published in 1969 by
EPWORTH PRESS

Book Steward
Frank H. Cumbers

Printed in Great Britain by
Page & Thomas
The Chesham Press Ltd., Chesham
Buckinghamshire

SBN 7162 0075 9—9

TO

ERNEST GORDON RUPP
President of the Methodist Conference 1968-9

Meditation, for a Young Boy Confirmed

I say to my son, these are the visible and outward forms,

These are the inarticulate gestures, the humble and supplicating hands of the blind reached out,

This is the reaching out of children's hands for the wild bird, these are the hands stretched out for water in the dry and barren land.

This is the searching in a forest for a treasure, buried long since under a tree with branches,

This is the searching in the snowstorm for a long-awaited letter, the lost white paper that has blown away,

This is the savage seeking a tune from the harp, the man raking the ashes for the charm in the burned-down house.

This is man thrusting his head through the stars, searching the void for the Incomprehensible and Holy;

Keep for it always your reverence and earnestness, these are men searching here,

They stretch out their hands for no star, for no knowledge, however weighty,

They reach out humbly, supplicating, not more than a cubit's length

That haply they may touch the hem of the robe of the Infinite and Everlasting God.

This kneeling, this singing, this reading from ancient books,

This acknowledgement that the burden is intolerable, this promise of amendment,

This humble access, this putting out of the hands,

This taking of the bread and wine, this return to your place not glancing about you,

This solemn acceptance and the thousand sins that will follow it, this thousand sins and the repenting of them,

This dedication and this apostasy, this apostasy and this restoration,

This thousand restorations, and this thousand apostasies,

Take and accept them all, be not affronted nor dismayed by them.

They are a net of holes to capture essence, a shell to house the thunder of the ocean,

A discipline of petty acts to catch Creation, a rune of words to
   hold One Living Word,
A Ladder built by men of sticks and stones, whereby they hope
   to reach the heaven.

Alan Paton

O lead my blindness by the hand,
   Lead me to thy familiar Feast,
Not here or now to understand,
   Yet even here and now to taste,
How the eternal Word of heaven
On earth in broken bread is given.

We, who this holy precinct round
   In one adoring circle kneel,
May we in one intent be bound,
   And one serene devotion feel;
And grow around thy sacred shrine
Like tendrils of the deathless Vine.

We, who with one blest Food are fed,
   Into one body may we grow,
And one pure life from thee, the Head,
   Informing all the members flow;
One pulse be felt in every vein,
One law of pleasure and of pain.

W. E. Gladstone, 1809-98

Contents

Contents

Acknowledgements

CHAPTERS two to seven of this book began as a course of
sermons preached on the Wednesday evenings of Lent 1968
to the Anglicans and Methodists of Southend-on-Sea. To
write up the rough notes I used then has brought back
memories of large and friendly congregations in fine
churches, who listened with much kindness. But the
treatment here is ampler and, I hope, in better literary
shape. These are devotional essays rather than sermons.
The prayers which follow the studies are intended to give
them direct personal application.

Alan Paton has kindly agreed to the extract from his
Meditation for a Young Boy Confirmed appearing as a
frontispiece. It is also found in Massey H. Shepherd Jr's
Holy Communion (SPCK). The Commandments are taken
from the Revised Standard Version of the Bible copyright
1946 and 1952. The quotation from Professor Jeremias on
p. 73 is from *The Prayers of Jesus* (SCM, 1967).

I am much indebted to Canon Jasper, the Church of
England Liturgical Commission and the SPCK for per-
mission to use the translations of the *Gloria in Excelsis*, the
Nicene Creed, and the Lord's Prayer published in *Modern
Liturgical Texts* (SPCK, August 1968). The Oxford
University Press has allowed on p. 17f. the extract from
Nathaniel Micklem's essay on The Sacraments in *Christian
Worship* (1936). He personally has consented to the quota-
tion from his *Prayers and Praises* (second edition 1954,
Independent Press) on p. 55. I would gladly give all the
rest of the book to have written those two passages.

GORDON S. WAKEFIELD

Harpenden, Hertfordshire
Feast of the Transfiguration 1968

ONE

The Christian Mystery

THE Fourth Assembly of the World Council of Churches
in July 1968 met in a fine new sports stadium at Uppsala,
the ancient Cathedral and University town in Sweden.
The main Fyris Hall was rectangular and of severe lines,
painted in pastel colours. Soft and gentle sunshine would
have streamed in on the fine days had there not been a
partial blackout and the harsh artificial lights of television.
The large Oikoumene symbol of the World Council, done
in copper and somewhat unintelligibly adapted to represent
the Christian's 'involvement' in the world, dominated a
building which was as typical of our age in its 'seculariza-
tion' and its cult of hygiene and physical fitness as could
have been desired. It was perhaps a little incongruous to
debate the terrible issues of Viet Nam, Nigeria and world
hunger in such healthful conditions, but the Fyris Hall
was no Hilton; it simply gave us room to do our work with
the help of Swedish efficiency and sanitation, with a
maximum of convenience and the necessary minimum but
no gross superfluity of comfort. No new Puritan need have
felt stricken in conscience while the radicals could be happy
that our surroundings were 'contemporary', not least in the
pictures which adorned our principal eating-place.

A temporary experimental church had been erected in
the grounds of the Fyris Hall, a square wooden building
with some stained glass, but as adaptable for a discussion
group as for a Eucharist and with a large cinema screen
more conspicuous than a pulpit. Since this held but 200
people at most much of the Assembly's worship had to
take place in the Hall itself amid the apparatus of our

13

work. The daily acts of devotion according to various traditions seemed rarely to become genuine 'common' prayer and such numinous moments as we had were when Pete Seeger made us sing *Jacob's ladder*, the Salvation Army led us in some of its jolly Music Hall choruses and, above all, during Olov Hartman's drama of *Amos*, which, while fashionably censorious of the Church, used the Old Testament story to prefigure the mercy and judgement of Christ.

For my own part I needed to leave the Fyris Hall and go to the Gothic Cathedral for the full worship of God; to abandon the noise of discussion, the memoranda and mountains of typescript, the pressure-groups, the strident awareness of the world's news, the tyranny of the relentlessly moving hours, and the garish modernity for the perspective of the centuries and the slow ritual acts which conserve Christian experience from the first days until now. Not that the Cathedral services were entirely traditional. The really valuable experiments were undertaken there rather than in the temporary building at the Fyris Hall. There was much new music, weirdly modern in its dissonances, and, at the end, a most glorious service of praise, which combined liturgy and informality, things old and new, and used the whole vast interior of the Cathedral for movement and the uninhibited expression of faith and hope and joy. Not for one moment would I decry new and revolutionary forms of worship, great boldness in experiment, even with risk of failure, and the refusal to be confined to hallowed rites. We have built about the narrow way of true worship and made it a tunnel, whereas it should be open to the skies and to the vast expanse of God's world. And yet it *is* a narrow way which traverses the ages and goes on into the future towards the kingdom of God, rather than a broad way which takes in too much of any one passing age. That there must be traffic from the Cathedral to the Fyris Hall I did not doubt, that our orders of service must be relevant to our business agenda (which must be written by the world in which we live), I would heartily accept, that there is worldliness and evil in the Cathedral as well as outside, is beyond dispute, but I do not think that it is possible to see the whole world as the theatre of God's glory (a fine Puritan sentiment) unless somehow that glory is focused in particular acts which, though developed and enriched in the course of time, unite us with the very beginnings and age-long developments of God's purpose in Christ and bring us near to the very heart of the Gospel. At Uppsala, the Cathedral worship, the Swedish Lutheran Masses and the Orthodox liturgy, kept me sane enough to hear a word of God in the shrill protests of youth and to try to grapple realistically with our hideous times.

To this extent, the Assembly made more clear my long-held conviction that there can be no Church without worship. Christians today must be so activist in the fight against world poverty, racialism and war, that it ought not always to be easy to distinguish the Church from a humanitarian political party or an ecumenical Oxfam. But behind this there must be a hidden discipline, as Bonhoeffer knew, not advertised or displayed to attract customers, but quietly, incessantly, unselfconsciously pursued and, at its centre, the Sacrament of Bread and Wine, ordained by Christ himself. This may be truly celebrated anywhere, in upper room or cellar, by sick bed or on the battlefield, in a kitchen, or a sports stadium. There is no doubt that in the next period of Church history the precise surroundings and conditions may come to seem less and less important, but it is an especial privilege to worship in the Eucharist in a place 'where prayer has been valid'.

It is true that the modern reader of the Gospel cannot be as certain as his ancestors that Jesus intended the rite of the Upper Room to be repeated throughout all ages. He cannot be sure what that ceremony precisely was, though he knows that it was neither a High Mass nor a Methodist love-feast. He is not even able to establish an unbroken chain between it and the eucharistic practices of the second century. Many fascinating theories have been advanced, many interpretations given of the words of Jesus over bread and cup. But the celebration of this sacrament as the central act of Christian worship and therefore of the Church's life will be justified, not because of any impregnable certainty as to its origin, though it is clear that Jesus ate ritual meals with his followers and that the early Church 'broke bread', but for at least four reasons both principled and pragmatic.

(1) *It incorporates the essential elements of Biblical worship—thanksgiving*, both for creation and redemption; *remembrance*, the solemn recall of the mighty acts of God in history, which brings them out of the past into the present; *sacrifice*, the self-oblation of Christians on behalf of all men and nature, by their union with the one perfect sacrifice of Christ; and the *mystery of union with Christ*, through his sacrifice, and *with one another* in the sharing of bread and wine.

(2) *It is related at once to history and to the timeless.* Archbishop Brilioth of Uppsala, on whose grave a wreath was laid during the Assembly of the World Council of Churches, claimed that the fundamental difference between the Christian Eucharist and the pagan mysteries is that in the case of the latter 'the "past" is a cult-legend of Attis, Isis or Mithra, in which not even the best will in the world could find a grain of historical truth, in the other it is the story of a human life whose essential historicity no sane critic can for a moment doubt'. In reading, preaching and action, the Holy Communion takes us back to the Man of Galilee, the Jesus who was crucified outside Jerusalem, whom his first followers proclaimed as risen from the dead. It also confronts us with 'the historic Christ in his fulfilment', for in each Eucharist we recall the Christ of many

ages and traditions as he has been celebrated in hymns, prayers, architecture and art and in the diverse experiences of our differing temperaments and individual lives. If we are Anglicans or Methodists in the Britain of the 1960s we shall use words which convey Cranmer's belief in Christ at the time of the English Reformation, though possibly with some modifications and nuances inherited from the Oxford Movement. We shall sing hymns by Wesley, Bernard of Clairvaux or John Mason Neale which will convey the riches of other traditions and influences of Christ. And to this we shall bring the mind of our own culture and education from our mother's knee to the latest sermon we have heard or book read or the direct sense of his presence in our hearts. To this extent Christ transcends any one historical period and the forms and actions of the service join us with an innumerable host of all ages and in every land.

But there is more than this, for in ancient liturgies, as in the letter to Hebrews in the New Testament, there is enshrined the belief that as we commemorate the historic Passion of the Lord we are brought into the eternal order and share, while still on earth, in the perfect worship of heaven. Too often was this profaned by the desire for a localized, material presence of Christ in the Sacrament, so that the direction, so to speak, was all wrong, and the mystery was expressed in terms of Christ's descent to the earthly altar, rather than the 'lifting up' of the worshippers into the heavenly realm in anticipation of the fully triumphant Kingdom of God.

This has never been expressed more powerfully than by the English Congregationalist, Dr Nathaniel Micklem, in the final words of an essay written in 1936:

According to the ancient use the minister at the Sacrament cries, 'Up with your hearts!' and the people respond, 'We lift them up unto the Lord'. From that moment it is conceived that the heavens are opened, and the Church on earth gathers with the Church in heaven—'therefore with angels and arch-angels and all the company of heaven we laud and magnify thy glorious Name'. So, too, time is, as it were, rolled up, and that which in ordinary human experience we know as successive is seen in the eternal simultaneity of heaven. From the blood of Abel shed at the foundation of the world, through the sacrifice of Abraham on Mt Moriah to the holy Nativity of Jesus Christ, Immanuel, His sacred Passion, His Resurrection in victory, His triumphs in the Church, His coming again in power and great glory—the whole drama of Redemption is, as it were, present together before our eyes as visibly occurrent, and the promise of our own inheritance is sealed by the Lord Himself upon our wondering hearts.

(3) *The Lord's Supper has both earthiness and mystery.* The Communion is a symbolic meal, whose elements are, as has so often been pointed out in the last thirty years, the products both of nature and industry. They represent not only the good gifts of God for man's sustenance and delight, but also the whole complex of commerce and of the evils and inequalities of our economic system. Some Christians indeed would be quick to seize on the degrada-tion and misery caused by wine and man's dependence on drugs for ecstasy and this should not be ignored in our sacramental meditation. But even more should we remem-ber that beneath the table, like Lazarus, full of sores, are the majority of our fellow creatures with whom we are not sharing bread, because of personal greed and thoughtless-ness and the wrong organization of our society.

It is felt today that the Communion is best celebrated in a light and airy building with the Table in the midst and the people round it and the minister central behind the Table, facing the people, not because he is so important, but because he is there to dispense the word and sacra-ment and should be within the circle, clearly heard and seen. The people come not as a collection of separate individuals but as the family of God. They should be able to recognize each other's faces, which to them are as the face of Christ, and to know a reconciliation which goes with them into the world. There is to be no mumbo-jumbo, no superstitious fear, but words which can be understood, and a joy and confidence in Christian fellowship. Perfect love has cast out fear of the wrath of God and man alike. One with our brethren in Christ, there is no evil that we cannot fight, no harm that we cannot withstand, no pain or terror that can divide us eternally. It is all related to the secular. As Professor von Allmen has said, 'The authenticity of Christian worship is not measured by Sunday, but by the period from Monday to Saturday'. The family circle of Christians in Church must not be broken outside, but rather widened to include all men everywhere. If I have received the bread and wine on Sunday, I must regard it as my mission to give it spiritually or materially to those whom I meet in my daily life, to bring them into the circle of those who partake of Christ, possibly because they are led to join the Church at the Holy Table and to definite and conscious commitment to him, but more likely because they are given his mercy and his peace where they are and in their worldly relationships.

And yet the mystery of Holy Communion concerns more than our life with other people in our mundane responsibilities. 'Things are not what they seem.' This is a sacramental universe and the phenomena of nature and the events of history are significant of more than can be conveyed by the physical account of them. They point beyond themselves to a transcendent mystery. The rainbow is caused by the refraction of the sun's rays on a cloud, but to the ancient Hebrews it was a sacrament of God's mercy, and to the Christian Platonist a source of unending wonder and joy, symbolic of the poetry in things. The water which David's valiant friends brought back to him from the well of Bethlehem at peril of their lives was no longer plain water but the blood which they would have shed for love of him. So when the Lord took bread, and said, 'This is my body', and wine, and said, 'This is my blood', he was referring to the mystery of union with himself, in all the fullness of his power and love, made possible by eating and drinking in the company of this friends. The union is spiritual, transcending time and space and the limitations of our biological existence, and yet so close, so intimate and so real that the most carnal metaphors may be used to describe it. To the outward eye, a group of ordinary people consume scraps of bread and take sips of wine; but these elemental human acts done in remembrance of him bring them into the very presence of Christ and to the threshold of the Kingdom of God.

This is an awe-ful mystery partly because the glory of communion with Christ is so great, the wonder more breathtaking than the Eiger or the noblest music. But also there is, as, Kierkegaard said, 'an infinite qualitative distance between God and man' and though, in Christ, God is with us, this does not mean that the distinction is abolished or that nothing was needed to bridge the gulf save the birth of Jesus. In the Gospel accounts of the life of Jesus, there is friendliness and 'involvement' but also a strange and disturbing remoteness, a rejection of the world and human relationships as well as a compassionate acceptance of them. It is indeed in his love that God is 'other' than ourselves, the distance is the distance between the love which is essentially erotic and therefore self-centred and the love which desires nothing but the good of the beloved. This love therefore cannot tolerate evil and yet must recognize that, since freedom is the prerequisite of goodness, it is possible for the beloved to separate himself utterly from God by an irrevocable series of wrong choices. And so while the Sacrament brings us to the glorious mystery of knowing God in Christ and being caught up even into his divine life, it does not allow us to forget the mystery of evil, which also is cosmic in its scope.

Jesus comes as our eternal joy; he comes also as our judge. We tremble both with wonder and with fear, with the rapture of our union in his mystical body and with the awareness of our danger of everlasting separation, the agony of which is all the more intense because it is not omnipotent tyranny which judges but love.

(4) *The Lord's Supper is both corporate and individual.* We have already had cause to say something about the communal aspects of the Sacrament in relation both to the Church and the world. Every liturgy now emphasizes these, not only by frequent congregational responses, by which the prayers become the people's own, but by giving as many members of the congregation as possible a share in the conduct of the service and by sometimes making the sermon, if not a dialogue, the result of preparation in the community. It is felt in some quarters that the construction of liturgies should not be left to the liturgiologists, but should involve the worshippers too. But it has yet to be proved that great liturgy can be the work of a committee of experts, let alone of people of varying degrees of knowledge and understanding some of whom may have little sense of drama or of the art of language. Great music springs from innumerable sources and may include some downright and unashamed plagiarism, but it is composed by one creative artist, not a team.

There is also a modern fallacy that our most active participation always consists in doing or speaking. Clearly we need to have more movement in church than at any rate Protestants have been used to, and we must not deprecate the many attempts to draw people more fully into the action of the liturgy, though a great deal of the success of these will depend on how well they know each other outside worship. The Uppsala service to which I referred could well have been sheer confusion and chaos had it not occurred at the end of the Assembly, when delegates and others were used to being together in a

21

crowd and to worshipping both in set forms and less usual ways. Like extempore prayers most experiments are parasites on liturgy and both demand some acquaintance with it and come alive as alternatives to its presupposed discipline.

But often we participate most fully when we are silent and submissive. A powerful sermon may be more successful than any number of responses in making a varied company of individuals as one. There was an old Breton peasant, who spent hours on his knees before the Blessed Sacrament in his village church. They asked him what he did all the time and he replied simply 'I look at him; he looks at me'. He was certainly one with Christ in a way most of us glimpse but from afar.

The Eucharist is a corporate act and we must ensure that it is understood as such both in our ordering of worship and our stress on the social responsibilities which should be its consequence. But the piety of the Breton peasant is needed too. This mystery is God's offer to *me* and *my* response to him. The pronouns of the liturgy are mostly plural and if the Nicene Creed is to be said in its original form, '*We* believe' as in the experimental Methodist rite, then there will be but one place in most non-Roman orders where *I* am addressed or make answer as an individual; but that is all important—'The Body of the Lord Jesus Christ, given for *you* (meaning *me*, the communicant); The Blood of the Lord Jesus Christ, shed for *you*'.

One of the glories of this service is that within the community and discipline of the Church it has inspired so much personal devotion. To this, such an anthology as Massey H. Shepherd Jr's *Holy Communion* (SPCK Seraph Books) is a slight but precious testimony. Nor is this confined to so-called 'Catholic' Christians, as any student of the English Puritans well knows. This Service is an infinite treasure-house of meditation, or, better, it is like some

tremendous magnet which can draw all ideas and specula-
tions to itself. Start with any text or passage of Holy
Scripture and it is possible to be led to some part of the
Holy Eucharist, to the mystery of Christ here displayed.
Any preacher at the liturgy, who expounds, as he should,
the Old Testament, Epistle or Gospel prescribed for that
Sunday, will find no difficulty at all in relating the chosen
portion to the celebration of which his sermon is a part, to
the sacramental gift and its receiving.

In literature and life as well, all roads may lead to the
Table of the Lord. E. M. Forster's *Where Angels Fear to
Tread* is the story of an Edwardian middle-class family,
whose widowed daughter-in-law makes an ill-advised
second marriage while on holiday in a small Italian town.
After months of disillusioning incompatibility with a man
of so different a background, she dies in childbirth. Her
first husband's brother and sister and a young woman
neighbour go to Italy to bring back the baby she has left.
In their clumsy efforts the child is killed.

The Italian father, violent with grief, attacks the already
injured English brother-in-law. Caroline Abbott, the
neighbour, manages to tear them apart. They both lie
panting, the Italian clutching her like a broken-hearted
child, when the housekeeper, who does not know what has
happened, brings up the baby's milk. Miss Abbott orders
the Italian to take the milk to the Englishman and per-
suade him to drink. When they have both obeyed, she
makes the Italian finish what is left. '*For she was determined to use such remnants as lie about the world.*'

Does not that take us straight to the one who made his
cowardly and acrimonious followers eat bread and drink
wine as a means of their reconciliation in him? Is he not
also 'determined to use such remnants as lie about the
world'?

The Eucharist has attracted to itself the riches, not only
of prayer, but of music and of art. The Roman Catholic

theologian Eugene Masure, has claimed that 'the Mass, considered as a work of ritual art, is a pure masterpiece of tranquil beauty. Colour, sound, movement, all the aesthetic resources of the human body in its symbolic actions, are united and bound together in a context of splendid, stylized archaism around this altar . . .'. Today many Roman Catholics are aware that this aesthetic development may conceal the essential meaning of the service, may be, as Bernard Manning would have said, 'not so much a painting of the lily as a varnishing of sunlight'. All we need for the Sacrament is a Table, with Bread and Wine and a company of Christ's followers, one of whom may be specially appointed to lead the action. This action is in two parts: the Word, which consists in the reading and exposition of those sacred writings which are the records of Christ's life and through which he still speaks, and the Sacrament, which follows the simple pattern of the Upper Room when Jesus *took* bread, *gave thanks*, *broke* it and *gave it to his disciples*. Nothing more is necessary save the desire to recall him.

Yet clearly more is inevitable except on occasions of greatest emergency. As this bare outline is meditated and becomes meaningful, additions will be made and it will attract to itself every type of devotion, and artistic expression. It will be the great opportunity for intercession, for remembrance not only of Christ but of his people and his world. It will indeed be the supreme occasion of Christian prayer of which our private prayers are the extension. God's demands will sometimes be remembered as well as his offer; we shall want to acknowledge our sins and receive again his pardon. In a sense the bare celebration of the Lord's Supper does all this, but sometimes we shall need to make it specific and seek in advance the verbal assurance of forgiveness which the receiving of the sacrament seals. There is the matter of preparation too, of the manner of our approach and of the content of our praise.

The meditations contained in the following chapters are based on prayers and passages of Scripture which have a long eucharistic history, particularly, though in most cases not exclusively, among Anglicans and Methodists. They are likely to survive the revisions of this decade, though they may well in the future be permissive rather than mandatory. Each of them—even the Lord's Prayer—could be omitted without invalidating the service. On the other hand, at least three of them have importance quite apart from the Holy Communion. To think about them should both bring us to the coasts of the sacramental mystery and help us better to understand what it means to follow Christ in the whole of our lives.

TWO

The Collect for Purity

Almighty God,
unto whom all hearts be open,
all desires known,
and from whom no secrets are hid:
Cleanse the thoughts of our hearts
by the inspiration of thy Holy Spirit,
that we may perfectly love thee,
and worthily magnify thy holy Name;
through Christ our Lord. *Amen.*

THIS collect is a translation by Thomas Cranmer (1489-1556) of a prayer in the *Sarum Missal*, a medieval service book emanating from Salisbury, which made certain modifications in the Roman Mass and had great influence upon the first English Prayer Book of 1549. These days fewer people treasure our links with the past or find particular thrill in the thought that they are using words which bind them to their fellow Christians throughout the ages. This is an unfortunate consequence of our style of life, and one of the ways in which the Church must serve the *present* age is by appealing to the past against the excesses of contemporary arrogance.

In the Sarum rite, the collect is to be said as part of the preparation for the service, by the priest alone. It precedes a rather lengthy act of penitence.

Today one imagines that in none of our churches is preparation for Holy Communion so thorough as it used to be. 'Let a man examine himself before he eat of that bread and drink of that cup.' The words of St Paul were taken very seriously by the Puritans. In the Presbyterian

Churches of Scotland, Communion Sunday was infrequent, but preceded sometimes by a whole season of preparation and the Scottish *Book of Common Order* (1940) includes a special service for this purpose. An Anglican layman of the early eighteenth century, named Robert Nelson, wrote that in anticipation of the receiving of the Sacrament, men should 'trim their Lamps, examine the State of their Minds, renew their Repentance, exercise their Charity, enlarge their Devotions, spiritualize their Affections'; and to this end, should retire for a while from business and pleasure. Modern Anglicans, according to Archbishop Ramsey, are more inclined to 'trip along' to their communion.

Some evangelicals would maintain that this is a dire consequence of more frequent celebrations. The Dean of an English Cathedral, where there is a daily Eucharist, told me that he did not like to communicate too often. Familiarity may cheapen the gift and frequency diminish preparation. Yet a more modern psychology would not necessarily endorse this, while the classic guides of every tradition would insist that the only adequate preparation is a life in Christ and have warned that it is a greater fault to disobey Christ's command to eat and drink than to omit some of the devotional exercises which full readiness would seem to require. One can become so entrammelled in preparations that one neglects the means of grace. In spite of the difficult parable of the man without a wedding garment, it is better to come to God ragged and in consciousness of need, than to try to make oneself worthy beforehand, for this is to attempt to do from one's own resources what God alone can achieve and would make the sacrament unnecessary. If I can make myself perfect, then there is no need of a sacrament.

Contemporary teachers would cast doubt on the value of overmuch self-examination and too many acts of penitence. They would use a fashionable term of abuse and refer learnedly and scornfully to 'pietism'. But they are worth heeding. What I feel most guilty about is not necessarily real sin, and to labour to induce feelings of shame is not necessarily genuine penitence. Sin is so much a matter of my social involvement. The whole human race is misdirected and astray, but it is futile to indulge in too much beating of the breast as though it were my greed which was the cause of world hunger, my aggressiveness which had resulted in Porton Down. I am, of course, psychologically maladjusted, biochemically unbalanced, with a will like putty, a mind like a sewer, and an ego blown up to bursting point. But though I ought to be aware of this and soberly realistic about myself, it does not help me to brood too much on my wretchedness or to stimulate the pangs of remorse. There is some truth in the criticism that Cranmer's service of Holy Communion is too penitential. A protest march may be a better act of confession than a lengthy devotional exercise, either before the Lord's Supper or in the course of it. What we need for the Sacrament is a recognition of our entanglement in an evil system and of the taint of sin, and then a look to God, a fixing of our hearts and minds on Christ's love and victory.

At the same time, it is good to review my life, not every day or week, but regularly; to enquire whether I am in any sense serving the Christian Gospel in the world or just absorbed in my own concerns, even though I may hold office in the Church of God. And there may be some particular preparation, which is required of me, not on my knees in private before God, but in some definite deed. Perhaps there is a quarrel I should try to make up, an omission to repair, an illicit relationship to sever. Perhaps I ought to change my job! Nearly always it will be a matter not only of 'the interior life', but of social behaviour, not resolve, but action. I shall have to go and do something or talk to someone.

Otherwise, this collect at the beginning of the service, said quietly and with neither perfunctory haste nor an unctuous drawl, could give us most of the preparation that we need.

First, there is the acknowledgement of God. Cranmer added a word, which is not found in the original when he addressed him as *Almighty* God. Christians have felt as instinctively obliged to pay compliments to God as lovers to their ladies. The name Mary, so thrilling if you are in love with her, so precious because of its associations, is not enough by itself. It must be *dearest* Mary, *adorable*, *most beautiful* and the like, possibly even *fabulous*, which is literally nonsense. So it is with our adoration of God. We are not content that his name, tremendous and ineffable, should stand alone. We say 'Almighty God'.

Perhaps the epithet has unfortunate connotations, as though we were invoking one who could intervene in the affairs of nature and of human life with naked omnipotence; change the weather or stop wars. Cranmer probably believed that; we cannot. We have learned that the only Almightiness we can honestly attribute to any God who really exists or reveals himself in Jesus Christ is the power of love. And since love never compels or else it would deny its own nature, its victory is affirmed by faith alone. Almighty God means Overruling God and the title is an act of faith.

There are those today, some of them Christians, who are honest enough to confess that faith in a personal God is not easy for them. They do us great service in that they warn us against limiting God to our own forms of experience even the highest. And yet, since it is through human personality that we are given our intensest life, may we not say that it is as we think of God as personal, though the thought is inadequate, that the transcendental truth about him and ourselves may be disclosed to us?

What follows in the prayer is tremendous and terrible,

yet very full of comfort. 'Almighty God, unto whom all hearts be open, all desires known and from whom no secrets are hid.' 'There is nothing in creation that can hide from him; everything lies naked and exposed to the eyes of the One with whom we have to reckon.' There is no deceiving God! This frightens, yet reassures us. Before him there is no need to act a part as we must sometimes even before our dearest friends. We do not fear exposure—God knows already. And although he knows the bad, which is so much worse than even our most jaundiced self-examination brings home to us, he knows also the good, which we cannot possibly assess either.

But the searching glance of God does make us feel shabby. Like the sunlight, it shows up the dust and cobwebs; like an X-ray it reveals the canker and rottenness. And so we cry, 'Cleanse us . . . cleanse the thoughts of our hearts', and perhaps, even as we do so, we wonder if all the perfumes of Arabia will be sufficient for the task.

The very terms of the request show what kind of cleansing will be offered. 'Cleanse the thoughts of our hearts by the inspiration of thy Holy Spirit.' Cranmer does not translate the Latin of Sarum literally and I think that his rendering, whether intentionally or not, is of the profoundest importance. The original says 'by the infusion of thy Holy Spirit', almost as though the Holy Spirit were a supernatural penicillin with which we could be injected and the virus of impurity destroyed. But is sin best thought of as an infection,

> The seed of sin's disease,
> Spirit of health remove . . .?

Is it not, as the collect says, a matter of the 'thoughts of our hearts', which means the whole activity of our lives, the motions of the mind resulting in evil action, though only part of the nastiness we think ever becomes deed?

And purity is not cleansing from a taint, 'out, out damned spot', it is single-heartedness and freedom from the distractions and allures of sin.

What saves us from sin is a new inspiration. As we said earlier, self-examination, penitential exercises, spiritual ablutions may make us worse. But to be possessed by the Holy Spirit, to be thrilled with the possibilities and glories which are ours in Christ, cleanses us by lifting us into a new dimension and turns our minds and imaginations away from evil, so that it seems to belong to the dead past of our lower world and we are so absorbed by Christ that we have not time to think of it.

This is not to deny that discipline has a place. We are so much a unity of body and mind that our behaviour is often governed by physical and chemical reactions and—quite apart from our concern for the hungry—there is a Christian way of eating and drinking, and to fast in Lent may help to overcome our lusts and concentrate our minds wonderfully and even prepare us for the Holy Spirit. But it is inspiration we need, ecstasy, which means to stand outside ourselves. Everyone realizes this, which is why so many people seek the bogus ecstasy of drink or drugs. 'Do not give way to drunkenness and the dissipation that goes with it, but let the Holy Spirit fill you.' The power which flows from the life and death of Jesus, the power, which, so Christians believe, is the source of this vast mysterious universe will take possession of us if we open our hearts. Perhaps, as Bonhoeffer saw, we need to renounce any attempt to make something of ourselves, and as we are fully and freely engaged in this world, evading neither its responsibilities, relationships nor true delights, to share in the community of those who keep alive the memory of Jesus. Then in the environment of Christian faith and living tradition, we need but one prayer for ourselves:

Come, Holy Ghost, our hearts inspire.

This is the way to cleansing, and more, to perfection. 'Cleanse the thoughts of our hearts by the inspiration of thy Holy Spirit that we may perfectly love thee and worthily magnify thy holy Name. . . .' The prayer is redolent of what has been called 'the optimism of grace'. Once we are possessed by the Holy Spirit there is no need to set any limits on the possibilities of our love or the value of our worship.

It is not presumptuous to pray that we may *perfectly* love God in the service for which this collect is the preparation. The Holy Spirit unites us to Christ and the act of thanksgiving in which we are to join is his worship and not simply ours. It is the service which brings before us his own great act of praise in the sacrifice of the cross and makes us sharers in it. We love God perfectly in him.

As far as our own state goes we are still imperfect mortals. But we ought not to think of perfection as a state so much as a process. In our worship in this world we clearly have not reached the final goal of the Christian life, but we are on the way to it and in the inspiration of the Eucharist we may love God as perfectly as at this stage of our journey is possible.

We noted at the beginning that this prayer was originally part of the priest's preparation for the Sacrament. Does the minister need more preparation than the people? Is not this a fallacy of that disastrous clericalism which has assailed all Churches and which the true understanding of the Church as the people of God and the Sacrament as its celebration, destroys?

Any notion which surrounds the minister with an ethereal glow or which makes him more than a man is pernicious. No more than the congregation can he make himself fit for his task and he will often need to take refuge in the thought that, through the mercy of God, his evil heart does not invalidate what he does. He will often be distressed by his knowledge of himself—his lack of feeling, of response to the wonder of the Gospel, his worldly standards and carnal thoughts, his failure to master himself. But so will any other worshipper.

And yet the minister has a special function in the Body of Christ and a distinctive task on behalf of the people. He is often their spokesman, to God as well as to men. He is set apart to give his time and his mind wholly to the direct work of the Church (a comprehensive term which means everything from the *opus dei*, the work and worship of God and the study of theology, to what Charles Smyth once called 'the blessed drudgery of visiting old ladies with bad legs'). Therefore as a matter of sheer practicality, he is able to co-ordinate the prayer and worship of the people of God, to see them steadily and to see them whole, and present their offering. Neither is it blasphemy to go on to say that the minister, like the apostle stands in Christ's place as he proclaims the word of reconciliation and invites men to the Table of the Lord. One appropriate symbol of the meaning of Christianity could be a man kneeling at a Table and then rising and bidding people come and receive. Sometimes the isolation of ministry may need to be stressed. The prophet may be alone, 'over against' men, even religious men, while the priest is the guardian of a truth, the conserver of riches, which the generality of mankind, even in the Church, may misunderstand, deny or prodigally cast away. The minister is often a caricature of prophecy and priesthood, as narrow, authoritarian, unimaginative, ignorant and exhibitionist as most men, if not more than most. And yet it has usually been through, at any rate 'the remnant' of the ministry, that the true faith has been maintained and Church and world have been renewed.

But this is properly a prayer for minister *and* people, best said together, though sometimes the congregation may enter more into the spirit of a prayer by listening as it is said for them. It comes at the beginning of the Eucharist, the great service of thanksgiving. It asks that we may perfectly love God and worthily magnify his holy name as we remember Christ through the means he ordained. But it could almost as well conclude the Eucharist as a prayer for our continuation of worship in our life and work.

> Day by day, we magnify thee;
> And we worship thy name, ever world without end.

For Recollection

There is nothing in creation that can hide from him; everything lies naked and exposed to the eyes of the One with whom we have to reckon (Hebrews 4.13).

Thou art a God of seeing (Genesis 16:13).

> In all my vast concerns with Thee,
>   In vain my soul would try
> To shun Thy presence, Lord, or flee
>   The notice of Thine eye.
>
> Thy all-surrounding sight surveys
>   My rising and my rest,
> My public walks, my private ways,
>   The secrets of my breast.
>
> My thoughts lie open to Thee, Lord,
>   Before they're formed within;
> And, ere my lips pronounce the word,
>   Thou know'st the sense I mean.
>
> O wondrous knowledge, deep and high;
>   Where can a creature hide?
> Within Thy circling arms I lie,
>   Beset on every side.

34

So let Thy grace surround me still,
    And like a bulwark prove,
To guard my soul from every ill,
    Secured by sovereign love.

Isaac Watts (1674-1748)

For Meditation

Thou art a God of seeing

To God all hearts are open and he sees into them; but also he *fore*-sees, understands our situation, takes an interest in the whole of our lives and, if we will let him, goes before us and prepares our way.

We cannot take a mechanical view of his Providence (foresight) or believe that every detail of our lives is precisely mapped out—birth, friendships, illnesses, successes, failures, death. To the non-Christian belief in Providence may well be superstition; but a Christian, trusting in God, will believe that God will help him to use all the circumstances of life in the single-hearted following of Christ, which is purity.

Of this, the Cross is the measure and sometimes all God seems to provide are wood and nails and enemies and the time for sacrifice.

Then the Christian remembers his Lord and prays that in all time of his tribulation, in all time of his wealth, he may be united with the one sacrifice of perfect love.

Questions for Myself

Why should I be comforted as well as disturbed by the thought that I cannot hide anything—least of all myself—from God?

What in my past life and present circumstances seems to be the provision of a God who would lead me in the way of Christ?

THREE

The Commandments

THE TEN COMMANDMENTS

God spoke all these words saying, Hear the Lord your God;

You shall have no other gods before me.

You shall not make yourself a graven image,
or any likeness of anything that is in heaven
above, or that is in the earth beneath, or that
is in the water under the earth; you shall not bow
down to them or serve them.

You shall not take the name of the Lord your God
in vain.

Remember the sabbath day, to keep it holy.
Six days you shall labour, and do all your work;
but the seventh day is a sabbath to the Lord your God.

**Lord have mercy upon us, and incline our hearts to
keep these laws.**

Honour your father and your mother.

You shall not kill.

You shall not commit adultery.

You shall not steal.

You shall not bear false witness.

You shall not covet.

**Lord, have mercy upon us, and write all these thy [your] laws
in our hearts, we beseech thee [you].**

Our Lord Jesus Christ said: the first commandment is, Hear, O Israel:

The Lord our God, the Lord is one; and you shall love the Lord your God with all your heart, and with all your soul, and with all your mind, and with all your strength.

Lord, have mercy upon us, and incline our hearts to keep this law.

The second is this, You shall love your neighbour as yourself. There is no other commandment greater than these.

Lord, have mercy upon us, and incline our hearts to keep this law.

A new commandment I give to you, that you love one another; even as I have loved you, that you also love one another.

Lord, have mercy upon us, and write all these thy [your] laws in our hearts we beseech thee [you].

JOHN CALVIN seems to have introduced the practice of saying the Ten Commandments into the service of Holy Communion and Thomas Cranmer followed him in the English Prayer Book of 1552. Calvin soon abandoned the Commandments—in the Lord's Supper that is—but they have continued in the *Book of Common Prayer* and in the principal Methodist Order, which is so close to it, though it is fashionable in our century to replace them by Our Lord's Summary of the Law.

Students of liturgy are inclined to feel that the Commandments do not properly belong to the Communion Service. Both the Anglican and Methodist experimental orders make their use permissive, though the Methodists require the *Commandments of the Lord Jesus* on the first Sunday in Advent and the Ten on the first Sunday in Lent.

Like everything that is customary, their recital in the Eucharist can be justified. They confront us, particularly in Our Lord's summary, with the standards of Christian behaviour at the outset of the service. And it is traditional to subsume the ten under the two and to think of the first

37

of Moses' tables of stone as containing the first four, which refer to love of God and the second as containing the last six, which apply to love of neighbour.

There are many these days who find the Ten Commandments an embarrassment, with their vengeful and jealous Yahweh. No twentieth-century Christian congregation is happy with the full version of *Exodus*, spoken by one who visits the sins of the fathers upon the children, even though this is what seems to happen in human experience. But we recoil from attributing what may be a 'law of nature' to the direct fiat of God.

What this crude and graphic pronouncement affirms is that law is God's gift. It is a fence against the ever-encroaching jungle which would destroy the life of man without it. Even 'an eye for an eye and a tooth for a tooth' is better than two eyes for one, or a whole jawful of teeth, which is what unrestrained human vengeance would demand. Law protects and although too relative for us to believe as the Jews did, that God dictates or writes its every letter, we may well hear his voice in the gropings of communities as they search for good order and large justice.

Law guarantees liberty, in the sense that to accept it and live by it is a release from the sometimes crushing bewilderment and responsibility of having to find one's own way in the world without signposts or maps. Law gives guidelines for action and personal dealings, whereas otherwise we might be utterly lost in the maze of things. We can often rest in the commandment as an empirical solution of a problem, instead of having each time to start from the beginning and resolve the matter for ourselves. This, I suppose, is how science is free to advance. Fresh discoveries are made on the basis of old 'laws'. The researcher does not continually have to go back and do all the previous experiments. Even more pertinently, the 'paternalism' of law, like a parent's guidance and discipline of a child, is very merciful. It saves the child from the complex responsibilities of adult life before he is ready for them. Without rules and guidance the child's growth would be stunted and he would be driven to despair.

And yet law has its limitations.

(1) It states what is the rule, but does not give reasons for it. Indeed, one must not reason with the law, as any one has tried to argue with a policeman about a traffic offence knows, probably to his cost; one must simply submit. The only question allowed in court is 'What is the law and has the defendant broken it?', not 'Why this law?' Sooner or later this will not satisfy the restless mind of man. In our own time, even the most sacrosanct laws are questioned. There are some who ask, and we must not number them all as libertines desiring free rein for their lusts, 'Why should marriage be of one man with one woman for life?' It is not enough simply to say 'This is the law', because it has not been so everywhere and at all times. There must be justification in terms of human personality. In the case of marriage, this will not be difficult. Monogamy and absolute fidelity within it, would seem to be the truest way to honour human love and bring it to perfection. The alternatives often do violence to human personality and injure it beyond repair. Yet there are exceptions and sometimes the only way to save personality is to admit that love is dead without hope of resurrection. But this is probably less often the case than fashionable opinion tends to think.

Sometimes a law cannot be justified. The early Christians, or at least the most understanding of them, discovered that Christ had set them free of much of the Jewish law—circumcision for instance. They even revised the Ten Commandments by making the first day the Lord's Day in place of the seventh. Sabbatarianism, the application of the Old Testament Sabbath laws to the Christian Sunday, was probably a mistake of well-meaning legalists in both the medieval and Protestant Churches.

In the early years of the Reformation, the Romans were the sabbatarians rather than the Protestants. William Tyndale even went so far as to say, in reply, be it noted, to Sir Thomas More:

We be lords over the Sabboth; may yet change it into the Monday or any other day as we see need, or may make every tenth day holy day if we see a cause why. We may make two every week if it were expedient, and one not enough to teach the people. Neither were there any cause to change it from Saturday than to put a difference between us and the Jews, and lest we should become servants unto the day, after their superstition.

Tyndale does not say that no special time for worship and teaching is necessary. In our day Christians will probably need to learn more than ever how to live by rule; but the rule will not be the same for every Christian. Temperament and stages of religious experience must be reckoned with, while in an age when automation may obliterate the distinction between day and night, and has already gone far towards destroying the old pattern of the seven-day week, uniform observance becomes impossible.

And the Christian rule cannot be imposed on society at large. Those of us who know Christ must worship and learn of him; but we must not do so in a spirit of Pharisaic superiority or in condemnation of those of our friends and neighbours who do not share our faith.

(2) Law can induce a wrong sense of guilt. We may be crushed and humiliated because we feel that we are in the wrong against laws which are unreasonable or do not go to the roots of good and evil. The codes of unenlightened, if not misguided, social convention, or the prohibitions of severe parents may destroy our confidence for life. And so we are made defensive and guilt-ridden, over-apologetic, too ready to admit faults, with a sense of being always in the wrong, whereas we need so often to be bold and assured, free of inhibitions, prepared to enjoy ourselves

and to be masters of life, not slaves. Every psychiatrist knows that the guilt often *precedes* the crime. This may have been what Paul meant when he said 'I had not known sin apart from the law'.

This has ramifications of great subtlety. Sometimes what the law makes us ashamed of are not our real sins. Since law is based on what the consensus of opinion accepts, the first consequence of breaking it is a loss of reputation. And so, much of our fear may be of public scandal rather than sin, and our guilt be due to the loss of men's esteem, rather than alienation from God, or an understanding of our wickedness and sorrow for it.

Yet even the imperfections of the law may bring us to Christ and be, as Paul said, like the surly slave who took the unwilling Roman boy to school. The Uppsala Assembly was much preached at and hectored by rather humourless young people, whose religion seemed all law and no grace; a constant telling of their elders where they had failed and what they were to do. They were a great irritant and yet who could say that they were not perhaps 'a kind of tutor to conduct us to Christ' by reminding us, though one-sidedly, of some of the priorities of our world, which Christians, preoccupied with ecclesiasticism, may ignore.

In our private lives, a nagging conscience, even if it is not awakened to our real sins, may show us that we are ill-at-ease with life and in need of true repentance and conversion. Then, in Christ, we find the only confidence, which cannot be destroyed, the confidence which rests in him and on his power and love, not on ourselves. This was the confidence of Bonhoeffer. Whether he was right to become allied with those violent men who conspired to assassinate Hitler (and break the sixth commandment) is a matter about which Christians and others will dispute for a long time to come. Where he was justified, is in his words near the end, 'My past life is abundantly full of God's mercy, and, above all sin, stands the forgiving love of the Crucified'.

(3) Law limits attainment. The classic instance of this is the rich young Ruler. He was able to say that he had kept the commandments from his youth and yet he refused Christ's summons to perfection. The law, which had protected and guided him and helped him to grow to maturity was now a cage, in which he was like a chained eagle. The law, which guards us so securely up to a point, may become a barrier against Christ and the daring adventure of the free sons of God. This was why Jesus restated it in the Sermon on the Mount:

You have heard that it was said to the men of old, 'You shall not kill; and whoever kills shall be liable to judgment.' But I say to you that every one who is angry with his brother shall be liable to judgment. . . . You have heard that it was said, 'You shall not commit adultery.' But I say to you that every one who looks at a woman lustfully has already committed adultery with her in his heart.

Jesus did not only intend to show us the depth of sin and make us miserable suppliants for mercy, but to point us to a perfection, which the observance of the law can never yield. It is hardly possible to legislate against motives unless they become outward acts. Murder can be condemned, but not the hateful thought. If you manage to restrain your fist from injurious or fatal blows, it does not matter how much you clench it, or what you feel in your heart; you are safe from the law. But you are not a Christian.

Christ offers not a new law, but a new life; not simply the power to keep the commandments, but to live in response to love. This is what he means when he sums up all in love, as Paul does after him. 'Love is the fulfilling of the law' and for our definition of love, we should go to 1 Corinthians 13, which is Paul's life of Jesus.

This love is our response to what God has given us in Christ. 'We love because he first loved us.' And out of love we keep law, which means that we submit to the rules of society, unless they are palpably unjust and iniquitous, and govern our own conduct by concern for other people. But this now becomes no longer duty but delight.

The difference is obvious. No man will be perfectly content if his wife stays with him simply out of a sense of duty. Sometimes duty is better than divorce; sometimes in acute temptation it may sustain us and bring us through the cloudy and dark day. No Christian will ever find himself able to despise law or to abandon it lightly. But nearly always law is an average, and duty a minimum. Love alone is sufficient, that compulsive, irrational force, which changes with the years but only that it may deepen so that a couple should say at their silver wedding that they love more not less. The bloom of youth may have departed, but the richness of personal relationship should have increased and the failures, sorrows and even sins of the years should have strengthened love. This is 'the fulfilling of the law', which is completed, perfected, transcended in love.

And love will always seek to make law wiser and more humane. The saints, the great lovers of God and man, are *above* the law, not content to live by the social mean or the finical rubric. But their heroism, their self-abandon has its consequences for good even in this world and gradually, agonizingly lifts society and its rules to a higher plane.

But this does not imply that the 'Thou shalt not' of the ten commandments is altogether superseded. Sometimes love involves negatives—a saying 'No!' There is in Christianity denial as well as affirmation. 'If any man will come after me let him deny himself and take up his cross and follow me'. Some of us can only enter into life maimed and will be saved because of the 'Thou shalt not'.

There is always the need for obstinate men of principle, who are not time-servers, but obey conscience, whatever the cost. One thinks of Sir Thomas More, as he is portrayed in the play and film *A Man for All Seasons*, the title of which means that he was invariably a pleasant companion, not that he veered with the political and religious climate. Far from it! But he did not expect others to conform to his conscience on the particular issue which cost him his life. (It is fair to add that More was hardly an apostle of toleration and, as the play vaguely suggests, was hot against heretics.) The individual Christian will not demand that others, even of his own faith, will necessarily accept the negations which are right for him, and he will be open to the advice of those of his fellow believers, who may try to show him, in the light of Christ, that he is over-scrupulous. But when all is said about 'holy worldliness' and life for living and even the supreme rule of love, it is sometimes love itself which calls us to take up the cross and have no more liberty on earth than did our Lord as he moved along the *via dolorosa* and bore the full weight of the law on Calvary.

For Recollection

I will run the way of thy commandments: when thou hast enlarged my heart.
Thy statutes have been my songs in the house of my pilgrimage. I see that all things come to an end: but thy commandment is exceeding broad. (Psalm 119: 32, 54, 96).

Love is the fulfilling of the law. (Romans 13:10)

> The thing my God doth hate
> That I no more may do,
> Thy creature, Lord, again create,
> And all my soul renew.
>
> My soul shall then, like Thine,
> Abhor the thing unclean,
> And, sanctified by love divine,
> For ever cease from sin.

That blessèd law of Thine,
Jesus, to me impart;
The Spirit's law of life divine,
O write it in my heart!

Implant it deep within,
Whence it may ne'er remove,
The law of liberty from sin,
The perfect law of love.

Thy nature be my law,
Thy spotless sanctity,
And sweetly every moment draw
My happy soul to Thee.

Soul of my soul remain!
Who didst for all fulfil,
In me, O Lord, fulfil again
Thy heavenly Father's will!

Charles Wesley, 1707-88

'Out of each Commandment I make a garland of four strands. First of all, I take each Commandment as a teaching, which is what it really is, and reflect on what our Lord God earnestly demands of me here. Secondly, I make a thanksgiving of it. Thirdly, a confession. Fourthly, a prayer.

Martin Luther, 1483-1546

Let us take the first commandment, as Luther says:
I am the Lord your God, who brought you out of the land of Egypt, out of the house of bondage.
You shall have no other gods before me.

(1) God has, in Christ, delivered us from the Egypt of Satan, Sin and Death and leads us, through the wilderness (where we have no permanent dwelling or changeless

institution) towards the Kingdom of his promise. He is the only one on whom we can depend. We must worship neither law, nor Church, nor spiritual power, nor creature, but God alone.

(2) Praise God for his victory!

> The day of resurrection!
> Earth, tell it out abroad;
> The passover of gladness,
> The passover of God!
> From death to life eternal,
> From earth unto the sky,
> Our Christ hath brought us over
> With hymns of victory.
>> *John of Damascus*, 8th century

Praise God, too, for the guidance of his law in the desert, where, otherwise we should lose our direction completely!

(3) Let each ask himself: What gods do I really worship? and make confession to God. Some idols are very obvious —money, pleasure, ambition, myself. But suppose law itself is an idol? Very few Christians understand what it means to be justified by faith. And in our Church life and our preaching, we offer law not grace. We nag rather than guide; we offend rather than comfort.

(4) I see the exceeding broad command,
>   Which all contains in one;
> Enlarge my heart to understand
>   The mystery unknown.

> O that with all Thy saints I might
>   By sweet experience prove
> What is the length and breadth and height,
>   And depth of perfect love!

FOUR

Gloria in Excelsis

Glory in heaven to God/Glory to God in the highest
and on earth peace to his people.
We praise you, we bless you, we worship you, we glorify you,
God of great glory, we give you thanks,
Lord God, heavenly king,
The Father, the Almighty.
Lord Jesus Christ, only-begotten Son,
Lord God, Lamb of God, Son of the Father,
you take away the sin of the world; have mercy on us.
You take away the sin of the world; receive our prayer.
You are seated at the right hand of the Father; have mercy
on us.
For you alone are the Holy one,
you alone are the Lord,
you alone are the Most High, Jesus Christ,
with the Holy Spirit,
in the glory of the Father. *Amen*

THIS hymn derives from the Eastern Church, where it belongs to Morning Prayer. Its use in the Communion Service is peculiar to the West, though very ancient, possibly
from the sixth century. It is a festal hymn reserved for the
most joyful occasions of the Church's life and tradition-
ally omitted in Advent, Lent and on weekdays.

It begins with the Angels' Songs at Bethlehem and thus
with one of the most familiar but difficult words of
Scripture and of worship—GLORY. This is a word which all
communions have in common. It is constantly used in
formal services, but would frequently be ejaculated by old-
fashioned Methodists, who, when stirred by sermons or

prayers, or sinners brought to repentance, would cry: 'Glory!'

Is it just an emotional noise?

'There's glory for you!' said Humpty-Dumpty.
'I don't know what you mean by glory,' said Alice.
'I meant, "There's a nice knock-down argument for you".'
'But glory doesn't mean a nice knock-down argument,' Alice objected. 'When I use a word,' Humpty said, in a rather scornful tone, 'it means just what I choose it to mean—neither more nor less.'

When we think about it, 'glory' seems to express a pomp and majesty, which most of our civilizations now repudiate and to point to a God who is like a tyrannical potentate of ancient times, demanding, for no apparent reason, a worship, which life in the world as we know it does not seem to make necessary.

The Biblical word, which has its origins in the Hebrew language, has two shades of meaning. First, it implies *distinction*, to which the idea of brilliant and dazzling splendour is closely related—a distinction which shines. 'There is one glory of the sun, and another glory of the moon, and another glory of the stars, for one star differs from another star in glory.' Each heavenly body is distinguished so that you cannot help noticing it.

Secondly, the word means *weight*, that which tips the scales in favour of distinction. We might say, for instance, that the glory of Chalfont St Giles is John Milton. Chalfont St Giles is a pleasant Chiltern village and local patriots might be prepared to claim on other grounds that it was unrivalled, but what tips the scales in its favour and means that there is nowhere quite like it is that Milton took refuge there from the Great Plague and there finished *Paradise Lost*. That gives it a weight of glory beyond all other places.

Believers claim that God is unique. 'To whom will ye

liken me and make me equal and compare me that we may be alike?' No human eye can see him or mind grasp his mystery. No analogy is more than imperfect; no vision gives more than the similitude of his glory or allows us to glimpse more than the outskirts of his ways. Philosophers —those who are not atheists—are not willing to admit that God is completely hidden in nature or entirely incomprehensible to the searching mind of man, but they affirm that communion with him demands a rigorous purgation and even when he is in some sense known, there remains an absolute, primordial, unfathomable mystery. But there is yet a more puzzling hiddenness. The glory of God is concealed because the world does not obviously bring him distinction, the scales are not tipped in his favour. At times an unearthly splendour shines through nature and men attain nobility and distinction by their sacrifices and achievements. There is a real, if intermittent, glory in the universe, but is it the glory of God? Often all is drabness and futility, if not horror, and the splendour passes away. There is little evidence of a glorious God anywhere.

The Christian answer is that the glory of God is seen only in Jesus Christ. The angels at Bethlehem could sing 'Glory' because that was its revelation. 'No one has ever seen God; the only Son, who is in the bosom of the Father, he has made him known.'

Christ is the King of Glory. The Divine splendour is not seen in portents and prodigies but in the love manifested in a carpenter turned preacher, who out of his own conviction about God, sought to bring life and liberty to men. The glory behind the shabby and mundane humanity of his career is exposed for a brief while when on a mountain top he is transfigured in the presence of his three most intimate disciples. But it is seen by those who really understand when he, the leader, washes the feet of his followers, and, supremely, when he dies amid the shame and stench of a crucifixion. And so the outburst of praise which uses every conceivable verb, 'We praise—we bless—we worship—we glorify . . .', goes from Bethlehem to Calvary and the Lamb standing as though it had been slain.

The Lamb is an ancient symbol of Christ, with Jewish antecedents, though the New Testament combines these with Hebrew ideas of sacrifice to take away sin and its defilement, not related to the offering of lambs. In Revelation, from which we have just quoted, Christ is the Lamb, not so much sacrificial victim as conquering victor, who has led the flock to battle and prevailed.

Is this any longer a 'charged' symbol? That we do not now in the western world live in a predominantly pastoral society is not the main objection. The rationale of sacrifice seems to us to be crude and sub-Christian, the imagery of the slaughtered lamb revolting. How can we in public worship invoke Christ as the Lamb?

Perhaps sentimentalists of an older generation find Katharine Tynan Hinkson's words still moving:

> All in the April evening
> April airs were abroad;
> I saw the sheep with their lambs,
> And thought on the Lamb of God.

The symbolism may live in that poem, as it does not in hymns on the Atonement and if so, we may be able to begin to recover its power, so that it makes possible what the Bishop of Durham would call the 'cosmic disclosure' necessary to its being appropriate language for worship today.

Abandoning the attempt to extract meaning from the Old Testament as the logical starting-point, let us see what the title Lamb of God could mean for us. We cannot strip ourselves completely free of the associations of our

50

cultural past, nor should we wish to do so, but they are like bells which reverberate only when we have found the hammer to strike them.

To call Jesus the Lamb is not, for us, to honour him. It makes us think of helplessness; there is pathos, not unmixed with amusement, though the creature inspires our tenderness and compassion. He is rather silly, but innocent and engaging.

Innocence which really has no meaning when applied to an animal—it is indeed an instance of 'the pathetic fallacy' —becomes almost frighteningly tremendous on those rare occasions when we encounter it in a human being. It is not simply that it overwhelms us by an almost supernatural power; we know that it is predestined to be the victim of the nastiness, the brutal cynicism of the impure.

Herman Melville, author of *Moby Dick*, wrote a last story called *Billy Budd*, which has recently been made into an opera. It tells of a handsome sailor, Billy Budd, who, though impressed into the Royal Navy from a merchant ship, does not bemoan his fate, but becomes the darling of the crew. There is one man who hates him, John Claggart, the master-at-arms. He accuses Billy Budd, falsely and preposterously, of conspiring rebellion. Budd is dumbfounded—we might say like a sheep before its shearers— but in the outrage of his innocence, his right arm suddenly shoots out and before anyone realizes what has happened Claggart has fallen to the deck, dead.

The judgement is inevitable. The just captain can but condemn Billy to be hanged at dawn. But as he dies 'the vapouring fleece hanging low in the east was shot through with a soft glory as of the fleece of the Lamb of God seen in a mystical vision and simultaneously therewith, watched by the wedged mass of upturned faces, Billy ascended; and ascending took the full rose of the dawn'.

There is a much fuller theological treatment of this novel

in F. W. Dillistone's invaluable little book *The Novelist and the Passion Story* (Collins, 1960). But such flimsy outline as I have given shows, I think, that when we seek to describe the encounter of innocence with evil, the Biblical imagery comes into its own.

This by no means exhausts the rich scriptural symbolism of the Lamb. To give but one further example, in *Revelation* it is declared that only the Lion of the tribe of Judah can open the seals of the book of history—but the Lion is in fact a Lamb, with the marks of slaughter upon him. Just as God's glory is perfectly revealed in the lowly Jesus, so his control of the universe is not that of hideous and tyrannical strength but of suffering love, which allows itself to be the victim of its own laws and conquers by assuming the burden of creation's woe. The innocent victim does for the rest of us what we cannot do for ourselves. He removes the sin inherent in the cosmos to where it can harm no longer. And his travail is the birthpang of a new world.

The *Gloria* provides our proper response to the work of Jesus Christ:

Lord God, Lamb of God, Son of the Father,
you take away the sin of the world; have mercy on us.
You take away the sin of the world; receive our prayer.
You are seated at the right hand of God the Father; have mercy on us.

There is no cringing servility in that. Jesus, the suffering Lamb, the sin-bearer, has conquered. He who submitted to the wrath of man and fought evil to the last by goodness and love is the remedy for the defilement of sin, and not simply the sin of those transgressions which we daily, hourly commit, but of that sin which we *are* because we are bound up in the frustration of the whole human race.

You take away the sin of the world; have mercy on us.

'The sin of the world' is more than the sum total of individual sins. It is the sin in which we would still be involved if our own private lives were impeccable. And this sin Jesus, Lamb of God, has taken away, not by some transaction which annuls our guilt, but by his own deed which results in the creation of a new humanity.

And yet there seems so little difference as a result of his life and death and exaltation. 'The sin of the world' seems as potent as ever. It will not indeed be until the end that Christ's victory is fully seen. We have to accept and live by it through faith. In the Church, amid the company of worshipping Christians, we affirm 'You take away the sin of the world' and we ask that his mercy may be given to us, so that we may be the pioneers of the new humanity, the motive of those whose every action is the love that we have received.

You take away the sin of the world; have mercy on us.

Let the mercy revealed in all that you have done be our glory as it is yours, so that, assured of forgiveness, we may be those whose light shines before men that they, seeing our good works, may glorify our heavenly Father.

Today we are told that our religion must be directed towards mankind and, it is suggested that there is really no difference between love of God and love of our neighbour. Indeed there are those who would seem to think that the glory of man should concern us more than the glory of God and that this is the real meaning of the life of Jesus. They have a case which seems especially strong against those who make pious and liturgical phrases an escape from hard thought or who take such lofty and patronizing refuge in terms which enshrine religious heights and depths which they themselves neither scaled nor plumbed.

But it is misguided to pretend that the Christian has no particular concern with the glory of God. Unless indeed there is a transcendent glory above all that we can ask or think, our human concerns and loyalties will become narrow, selfish and parochial, extensions of our own egoism, which as Henri Bremond said, it is one of the tasks of worship to disinfect. But more even than this, the Christian Gospel is not limited to the present age and life of man. It deals with those issues which no politics can resolve, those wrongs which no philanthropy can right, those matters of life, death and salvation which are beyond this world. It claims that Jesus has not simply a message of love and justice for the here and now, but that he reverses the whole thwarted history of the race and is the conqueror of the principalities and powers in the heavenly places and of death itself. This is why the *Gloria*, like the song of Bethlehem, proclaims both peace on earth and glory to God in heaven. The whole spiritual universe must reveal that his love is its distinguishing power and the balance of evil must be cosmically redressed.

What is the best place for the *Gloria* in the service of Holy Communion? In the Roman rite it has always been sung near the beginning, as in the English Prayer Book of 1549, and modern revisions restore it to this position. It is not inappropriate as a hymn of praise after confession of sin and strikes the note of worship, 'echoing angelic songs', at the very start. We prepare ourselves, perhaps receive the assurance of pardon, and then 'Glory to God!' We fix our eyes and minds on the objective work of redemption and on the Being in whom is all our hope and joy.

Yet Cranmer's 1552 placing of the *Gloria* at the end of the service must not be regarded as inept. It must be seen, liturgically, in the context of the full Prayer Book Service, which began with Morning Prayer. For this reason, Cranmer's desire for a hymn of praise after Communion could not be met by the *Te Deum* or *Benedictus*, which had already been sung. What better than to transfer the *Gloria in Excelsis*? But there is theological appropriateness too. We leave the Lord's Table for the world and although we have received Christ in all the tokens of his forgiveness and his sanctity, we are still members of a sinful race and we need to pray for that mercy which will help us to live in the power of him who has dealt, not with our wilful, personal evil only, but with the sin of the world. And, though we rejoice in the victory which we have commemorated and must continue, we never outgrow the prayer of the publican: 'God be merciful to me a sinner.'

Whatever its place in the liturgy, or however often or infrequently its actual words are recited, the spirit of the *Gloria* should inspire the daily thanksgiving of all Christians. Words which Nathaniel Micklem once wrote about the 'Glory be to the Father', the doxology, which we sing after the Psalms, could well be used of the *Gloria in Excelsis:*

Almighty God, our Creator and the Creator of all the ends of the earth, Source of all Goodness, Truth and Beauty, is himself also our Redeemer, for he was in Christ reconciling the world unto himself by the mystery of his life and Passion; and he it is, too, he the Creator and Redeemer, who has given himself to our hearts whereby our love answers to his immeasurable love. He is God, the eternal Source of life; he is one with his co-eternal Son, the Word, his uttered Thought; the Holy Ghost is the eternal life of God, being the love of the Father for the Son and the Son for the Father; three 'Persons', yet one, only, everlasting, ever-glorious God. To him was glory in the beginning on Creation's dawn, when the morning stars sang together and all the sons of God shouted for joy; to him is glory now from the Church triumphant in heaven and from the Church militant, straitened, persecuted, yet believing, on earth, and from all Creation, for the heavens declare his glory, and the cattle praise him upon a thousand hills. His Kingdom is an everlasting Kingdom, and to all eternity everything in his house shall cry, 'Glory'. The *Gloria* is not a formula; it is the triumph-song of the redeemed.

For Recollection

'We give thanks to thee for thy great glory'

The world is charged with the grandeur of God.
  It will flame out, like shining from shook foil;
  It gathers to a greatness, like the ooze of oil
Crushed. Why do men then now not reck his rod?
Generations have trod, have trod, have trod;
  And all is seared with trade; bleared, smeared with toil;
And wears man's smudge and shares man's smell: the soil
Is bare now, nor can foot feel, being shod.

And for all this, nature is never spent;
  There lives the dearest freshness deep down things;
And though the last lights off the black West went
  Oh, morning, at the brown brink eastward, springs—
Because the Holy Ghost over the bent
  World broods with warm breast and with ah! bright
    wings.

Gerard Manley Hopkins (1844-1889)

The same God who said, 'Out of darkness let light shine', has caused his light to shine within us, to give the light of revelation—the revelation of the glory of God in the face of Jesus Christ.

When we give thanks for the great glory of God, we give thanks for Jesus Christ.

> He laid his glory by,
> He wrapped him in our clay. . . .

God, help us to understand that the meaning of the worlds is revealed, not in a splendid vision, or a philosophy of life, or a discovery of science, but in a Man, with a face like all men's faces, not transfigured, but disfigured, not glorified with Moses and Elijah, but crucified between two thieves. Thus may we be bold to follow him, who now lives and reigns with thee and the Holy Spirit, ever one God, world without end. *Amen*

Let us examine ourselves and the life and worship of our Church to see if we are not, in fact, more concerned with 'the power and the glory' than the Cross.

Yet we must remember that there *is* glory, which, though hidden now in time, will be seen one day.

Jesus is no longer on the Cross, but is in the splendour of God.

In our worship, we not only remember his Passion and are present at Calvary, we enter the eternal order.

This is what we so often fail to understand or to experience. It is all mundane, which it should be, but not wholly.

Like Bunyan's pilgrims at the Delectable Mountains, we should in our worship look towards the Celestial City and see something like a gate and also some of the glory of the place.

We must give thanks for the wonder and brilliance and perpetual light of God's eternal kingdom.

But, in the end, we return to this world, which we have never left, '*that part of heaven where our lot is cast*', and remember Christ's words:

> *Let your light so shine before men that they seeing your good works may glorify your Father which is in heaven.*

The Christian must reflect the Divine glory, which means that in his person he ought to be attractive and not necessarily avoid gay colours or brilliant clothes—provided they are part of the expression of his joy in God and not merely the vain panoply of conceit or self-regard or inordinate sex. He must pray to be delivered from seeking his own glory. When men honour or praise him, he will be gratified and thankful, *but will always make an immediate inward offering to God.* God of great glory, we give you thanks.

FIVE

The Nicene Creed

We believe in one God.

We believe in the Father, the Almighty, maker of heaven and earth, maker of all things visible and invisible.

We believe in his only Son, Jesus Christ, the Lord,
    begotten of the Father before time began:
    God from God, light from light, true God from true God.
    He is one in Godhead with the Father; not made, but
      begotten.
    Through him all things were made.
    For us men and for our salvation he came down from heaven.
    By the power of the Holy Spirit he was born of the virgin
    Mary and became man.
    For us he was crucified under Pontius Pilate;
    he died and was buried;
    on the third day he rose from the dead
    in fulfilment of the Scriptures;
    he ascended into heaven and is seated at the right hand of
      the Father;
    he will come again in glory to judge the living and the dead,
    and his kingdom will have no end.

We believe in the Holy Spirit, the Lord, the giver of life;
    he proceeds from the Father and the Son:
    together with them he is worshipped and glorified:
    he has spoken through the prophets.

We believe in one holy, catholic, and apostolic Church.
    We acknowledge one baptism for the forgiveness of sins.
    We look for the resurrection of the dead,
    and the life of the world to come. *Amen*

DURING the ecumenical Methodist Conference at Oxford in 1951, a service was held in the University Church to commemorate John and Charles Wesley. The preacher was John Scott Lidgett, then aged 97. He entered by the north door, supported by two sticks and several dignitaries, his aged and emaciated face, rising shrunken from his red doctor's robes. Throughout the service he remained seated, but in the hymn before the Nicene Creed, he insisted on being raised to his feet. Like some old soldier, pulling himself to attention before the flag, he would, to the last, salute the great symbol of Christian faith.

Scott Lidgett had a particular devotion to the Nicene Creed. I rather think that the first time I heard its name was in a broadcast by him, when I was eleven or twelve years old. Clearly it had not been used in the worship I attended as a child. But, in spite of this, Scott Lidgett is not the lone refutation of the statement sometimes made by those who ought to know better, that Methodists do not acknowledge the creeds. We accept them as the summaries of the faith on which our Church is founded. As the *Constitutional Practice and Discipline of the Methodist Church* puts it: 'The Methodist Church claims and cherishes its place in the Holy Catholic Church, which is the Body of Christ. It rejoices in the inheritance of the apostolic faith, and loyally accepts the fundamental principles of the historic creeds. . . .'

In those Churches where Morning Prayer is still the rule, the Apostles' Creed is recited weekly, while the Nicene Creed is said whenever the full Order of Communion is used. In the experimental orders for Baptism and the Burial of the Dead, the Apostles' Creed is prescribed, while, as *The Scheme*, the final report of the Anglican-Methodist conversations is able to say, the Methodist Senior Catechism gives a fuller exposition of this than does the Anglican. The experimental Methodist Communion rite does however place the Nicene Creed at the beginning of the Lord's Supper, the second part of the Service, and makes it permissive, thus admitting that the symbol is best used among those convinced enough to be communicants, and not by them to be reeled off lightly on every occasion. The Service also goes back, as does *Modern Liturgical Texts* to the original form of the Greek—'*We* believe . . . .'.

There has been an increase in Methodist use of the creeds in worship in the last fifteen years, though it must be recognized also, that there is a feeling among many that the recitation of creeds is a formality alien to the authentic Methodist tradition of liveliness and spontaneity. Allied to this is the inveterate uneasiness of the more liberal Christian with dogmatic statements of any kind, an uneasiness which is now much publicized by the radicals in all the Churches.

A knowledge of history does nothing to allay this. To read of the intrigues and quarrels, which surrounded the formulation of the Creeds, and of the Grosvenor Square demonstrations and political pressures which accompanied the intense religious faith of their origin, is repellent. We judge the past by a perfectionism which we certainly cannot practise in our own discussions of 'faith and order', and in our attitude to the Church of previous ages we forget the doctrine of the incarnation, which we are always advancing in our current theories. The treasure of the gospel is contained in the earthern vessels of life in human history. The Church in much of its existence is the prisoner of the forms and fashions and the sins of the age. There is no escape as long as time continues and the Church is genuinely in the world. This should make us understand though not excuse the nastier episodes of Church history, and while we admit them with penitence, recognize that they are part of the 'scandal' of what we celebrate as the glory of the gospel—that it is concerned with men where they are, in this complex of time and change and fallibility. Amid all that is sordid and imperfect, there is the truth of God in Christ, handed on from age to age and rediscovered in forms new and old as the centuries pass and the life of man evolves into varied cultures. But only the most rigorously incarnational philosophy can accommodate the infamies of the Church from the Inquisition to the unholy wrangle at the last Leaders' Meeting or PCC, and there is much in the story of the Creeds which is unpleasant and disturbing.

The Creeds have sometimes been instruments of persecution, while an Anglican scholar has recently opined that Nicaea 'imposes a greater restriction of manoeuvring room upon the subsequent theologians than they ought to have been required to accept'. May not Creeds circumscribe thought, prohibit speculation and limit the discovery that God has 'more truth and light, yet to break out of his holy word'? May they not constrict thought, as laws sometimes do behaviour?

The language, too, seems remote from our ways of thinking. What does 'of one substance with the Father' mean? What is the 'substance' or 'stuff' of the Godhead? The new translation helps here when it says simply 'He is one in Godhead with the Father', but I doubt if modern critics will find this much more intelligible while it leaves us with the problem of the Trinity!

There is also the objection, which may be put in the terms of the old Puritans, that the faith of the Creeds is 'history-faith' and not 'saving faith'. It is possible to give intellectual assent to Christian truths, to be captivated by the fascination of theological ideas, while living a self-indulgent life, far removed from the demands of the Gospel. To accept the Christian world-view, even to love the Church, its traditions and its worship, is not the same as to be a Christian, completely possessed by Christ, one's whole life, thought and behaviour an active response to his love. 'Not every one who says to me, Lord, Lord, shall enter the kingdom of heaven, but he who does the will of my Father who is in heaven.'

These are formidable objections and cannot be denied. And yet I think there is a proper and responsible use of the creeds both in worship and in the Christian life and particularly of the Nicene Creed. It is called 'Nicene' because, as far as the words, 'We believe in the Holy Spirit', it represents the definition promulgated under the prompting of the Emperor Constantine, by the Council of Nicaea (325). Later, it was supplemented by the Council of Constantinople (381) and accepted in full by the Council of Chalcedon (451).

It was added to the liturgy by a curious series of isolated developments, beginning at Constantinople in a period of the most unsavoury intrigue, as early as the sixth century. In the West, it was adopted towards the end of that century in Spain, which, ever militant, inserted it in the Eucharist for the fortifying of the true faith and a defence against heresy. It was to be recited immediately after the breaking of bread and before communion. Charlemagne, two hundred years later, seems to have liked the Spanish custom and adopted it in his own chapel at Aix, in France, though he placed the creed in the position most familiar to users of the *Book of Common Prayer*, after the Gospel. It was not until 1014 that the Nicene Creed began to be recited in the liturgy at Rome. But this tortuous and chequered history does not, to my mind, invalidate the creed. Compiled in an atmosphere of bitter argument and political skullduggery, it may yet enshrine the truth. Inserted into the Eucharist for various reasons and with differing degrees of conviction, it may yet be capable of guarding and affirming, though its language be poetry rather than science, a philosophy for our time.

The great medieval cathedrals and parish churches

were not all reared in humble charity or without sordid commerce and factions; nor have they been maintained wholly in Christian love and peace. But they are works of human creativeness and monuments of faith, which are capable of bringing men to God. So the creed.

It is an ecumenical document, as J. N. D. Kelly has said, 'one of the few threads by which the tattered fragments of the divided robe of Christendom are held together'. Even so, the phrase 'and the Son', in the verse 'He proceeds from the Father and the Son', is an addition by the Western Church, not accepted in the East. (To expound the reasons for this would take us too far into technical theology for our purpose.) Yet no other form of words represents so adequately what all Christians believe.

This does not mean that they all interpret the Nicene Creed in precisely the same way. 'By the power of the Holy Spirit, he was born of the Virgin Mary,' for instance, is perhaps capable of varying explanations, while no doctrine of Atonement underlies the rehearsal of the facts of Christ's sufferings and death. No definition of the 'one holy, catholic, and apostolic Church' is, so far, accepted by all Christians.

This is part of the value of words. They are always a little ambiguous, susceptible of different shades of meaning to different people, while they make possible a basic unity of understanding and action. Complete doctrinal agreement and precision will be attained only in the perfect life of heaven, where we shall know as we are known; meanwhile, a great symbol held in common, capable of being used in a variety of ways is an inspiration and enrichment to all Churches. It is like a theme on which different variations may be played to give great music.

Like every other statement of Christian faith, the Nicene Creed is an expansion of the most ancient testimony of all —'Jesus is Lord'. Its primary intention was to safeguard belief in the uniqueness of Jesus and to explain his peculiar place in the scheme of things as one who is truly man and yet God.

This is far more than an academic exercise, a chess game with antique pieces. Perhaps the most popular philosophy is that which implies that there cannot be any real connexion between the Perfect, the Realm of Absolute Values and this fleshly, material, so obviously soiled, sinful and finite world. This is why, as we have already noticed, so many people are inclined to repudiate the creed without examination once they learn the story of its origin; others would go to the opposite extreme and simply ignore the unChristian wranglings and conspiracies and say that the Church in its authority and teaching office must be free from sin and error. Similarly, the great heretics have always implicitly denied either the divinity or the manhood of Jesus. No true man could be God; no perfect God could be man, born of a woman, tempted, dying. The heretics, followers of Arius, whose teaching occasioned the Council of Nicaea, explained Jesus as an intermediate creature, uniquely made by God in order that he could do the dirty work of creation and redemption and prevent the Absolute Divine Majesty getting his hands soiled in this world.

To this the creed replies that Jesus Christ, about whose historical existence and full humanity there is no shadow of doubt, is 'of one substance with the Father'. In Jesus, God himself, the Creator, the All-Perfect is involved in and committed to this world of time and change. If I may borrow the language of David Jenkins' *The Glory of Man*, to which I am much indebted: 'Transcendence' (God's otherness 'over against' the world) 'is no necessary bar to immanence' (God's dwelling in the world), 'materiality is no necessary bar to spirituality, and change and process are no necessary bar to absoluteness and fulfilment. In fact, man and the universe fit together because of the involvement of God to that end'.

Two corollaries of this, as Jenkins shows, are of the

64

utmost importance. One of them, since there is no discontinuity between Jesus and men, is the incalculable value of every human being. The other, since Jesus is God, who controls and orders all, is that we are not ultimately at the mercy of any of the forces of the universe, planets or demons or light waves or physical powers. The Universe is not itself divine and is open to the investigations of science and the development of technology, provided that these are undertaken with reverence and the utmost responsibility and seriousness, since the universe is created and sustained by the God whose Word is Christ.

Thus we should be chary of jettisoning the Nicene Creed, or joining in the specious clamour for its revision. The fault of Christendom was not that it affirmed the creed and supported it so resolutely, but that it failed to grasp the amplitude of its implications. Nevertheless, these were a pervasive influence on the culture of the centuries and created the climate in which science could live.

The creed is an intellectual statement, which makes a claim upon our minds. Its use in worship helps us to prove what the Jesuit modernist of the beginning of this century, George Tyrrell, called 'the prayer-value of dogmas'. This does not mean that we ought to try to find devotional help through symbols which our knowledge invalidates or our intellect makes intolerable. But we cannot truly love the Lord without our mind and to include the creed in the Holy Communion should help to save our worship from being sentimental, provided that it has gained the assent of our reason. At the same time, its presence in worship shows that Christianity is more than a function of the brain and when our minds have wrestled with the problems of philosophy, we may find them transcended in devotion. Worship is no more an escape from thought than it is from life. But it is possible, at any rate for some, to be led through thought to prayer. As we meditate on the Christian interpretation of the universe, we find ourselves in the presence of God, in a realm where words and mental concepts, like the notes and staves of music, are comprehended in a vast and overwhelming harmony. Some years ago, Austin Farrer wrote a profound little book called *Lord I believe— suggestions for turning the Creeds into Prayer*. The subtitle shows what we should try to do. And, perhaps, if we succeed, 'history-faith' will become 'saving-faith'.

There is an attractive explanation of the fact that the shorter and more ancient Apostles' Creed belongs to Baptism and the Nicene Creed to the Eucharist. It is that the latter, longer and more philosophic, betokens the believer's advance in understanding, his maturer faith. Perhaps this is so, although, in some ways, the Apostles' Creed is more difficult for modern man, and I, for one, could spare it for the Nicene. But the underlying point is a sound one. We ought to grow in our apprehension of Christian truth as the years pass and one Eucharist succeeds another.

This will not mean an end of doubt, and, for our encouragement we should remember that it has not always been the stridently dogmatic Christians so much as those who have reckoned most honestly with their uncertainties, who have been the best witnesses for Christ. S. H. Hooke, a notable scholar, once led a summer school at a time when his own faith seemed at a minimum. Yet it was to the *religious* value of these lectures that his students paid tribute. Perhaps it is sometimes by way of intellectual doubt, when we have nothing to hold on to but the outward forms of worship, that we pass from resting in the faith of the Church to deep personal conviction and commitment; from the 'we believe' of the Nicene Creed, to the 'I believe' of absolute trust in Christ and Christ alone.

Jesus, my God! I know His name,
His name is all my trust;
Nor will He put my soul to shame,
Nor let my hope be lost.

66

Firm as His throne His promise stands,
And He can well secure
What I've committed to His hands
Till the decisive hour.

Questions to be discussed with others or ourselves in the attempt to pass from thought to prayer

(1) What are the truths about God which most encourage us to pray?

(2) Try saying at odd moments of the day, the Jesus Prayer. '*Lord Jesus, Son of God, have mercy upon me*'. Say it sometimes quickly, sometimes slowly, sometimes take each phrase and meditate on it and fill out its meaning. After Easter (assuming you begin in Lent) ask yourself what is the result.

(3) Do you believe in the Church? List all the Church's graces revealed in history and today and see, if, as well as your faith, your love is not kindled too.

An Act of Faith

When we have left the Lord's Table and returned to our duties in the world
Lord, we believe; help thou our unbelief.

When we read the newspapers and our hearts fail us for the things that are, and are coming, upon the earth
Lord, we believe; help thou our unbelief.

When we see our loved ones suffer and can do so little to help them, and their distress separates them from us and irritation chokes our love
Lord, we believe; help thou our unbelief.

When we are made aware of children, deformed, epileptic, spastic and deprived
Lord, we believe; help thou our unbelief.

When we think of millions undernourished or diseased, or perishing in the violence of our times
Lord, we believe; help thou our unbelief.
When we remember a Church divided and ourselves so far from the kingdom of God
Lord, we believe; help thou our unbelief.
When we come to the great crises of life and have no clear vision of the end for which we were created
Lord, we believe; help thou our unbelief.

Forgive our lack of faith, but also our faith. We list your attributes and call you names and forget that you are no formula but the living God. It is not we who grasp you by our thoughts and words, or even our worship, but you have taken hold of us in creation and in Christ and will not let us go. Live in us, think through us, love in us, our God and our all, our God and our all, our God and our all. *Amen*

SIX

The Lord's Prayer

Father in heaven:
  Your name be hallowed,
  Your kingdom come,
  Your will be done,
    on earth as in heaven.
Give us today our daily bread.

Forgive us our debts, as we have
  forgiven our debtors.
And do not face us with
  temptation,
  but deliver us from evil

For the kingdom, the power,
  and the glory are yours now
  and for ever. *Amen*

Father in heaven:
  Your name be hallowed,
  Your kingdom come,
  Your will be done,
    on earth as in heaven.
Give us today the bread of life.

Forgive us our sins, as we have
  forgiven those who wrong us.
And do not let us fall in
  temptation,
  but save us from the devil

For the kingdom, the power,
  and the glory are yours now
  and for ever. *Amen*

SOME years ago there was a caving accident in the Mendips, and, one Sunday, a boy and his girl friend were trapped by a fall of rock. She had a weak heart and as they waited long hours for rescue, he realized that she was dying. He was no churchgoer and his religious sense had been dormant, but in the agony of the crisis he felt that he must pray with her. He did not know many prayers. There was the Lord's Prayer, of course, but the repetition of this had been a formality at school and it meant nothing to him. In the end, he used that medieval prayer, which tradition has ascribed to St Ignatius Loyola, Founder of the Jesuits, 'Teach us, good Lord, to serve thee as thou deservest . . .', and it was in sound of these words that the girl came to her end.

    That pathetic and moving story is a rebuke to the way in

which Christians have misused the Lord's Prayer, 'the greatest martyr on earth', said Martin Luther, 'for everybody . . . tortures it'. The young man recoiled from its formality and its thoughtless, ritual babbling. He also realized that he did not understand it. He was right to avoid it and to turn to a prayer which was intelligible to him.

In the early Church, the Lord's Prayer, like the Lord's Supper, was kept very much for Church members, those who had received the gift of the Holy Spirit, who belonged to the family of God, and could therefore say its opening words 'Abba, Father!' (Romans 8:15).

Of course, man has an instinct for prayer. As Bunyan said, even beasts and birds make noises when they want food, and man will cry out for the satisfaction of his needs, for help in distress and comfort in anguish. Sometimes, indeed, his prayer will be the expression of protest and complaint. He will lift to heaven, not hands placed piously together, but clenched fists. But for its full efficacy, prayer depends on the environment of what Christians know as *grace*, the activity of God, through Christ, in his people.

This helps us to understand the apparently puzzling and discouraging limitations of prayer. It is not always able, for instance, to reach the operative area of mental illness. Murderers have been known to pray that they might not commit their crimes, but without avail.

In a sense only Christians can truly pray, because they are, or should be, in the community of love and have received the healing of Christ. They have entered into that relationship with God, through which they may become the means whereby his love can reach themselves and mankind.

The Lord's Prayer must be the most difficult in the world to the non-Christian, the man or woman outside the Church. To the Christian, it will not always be easy, if only for the reason that it is the prayer of Christ's agony,

'Abba, Father . . . thy will be done'. But as he lives with it, in the trials of life and the comradeship of his fellow Christians, the believer will find that he will come to use it with the simplicity of a child. I want to interpret it in terms of three definitions of prayer.

John Cassian, one of the early founders of monasticism, said that *Prayer is the lifting up of the mind to God.* In the sixth chapter of St Matthew's Gospel Jesus teaches the Lord's Prayer to people who do not need to be persuaded that prayer is an important religious duty. They have been taught to pray from childhood and they believe in prayer, because, like the soldier who believed in Infant Baptism, they have 'seen it done'! Prayer is a performance, not so much addressed to God as exhibited to man. To them, Jesus says, 'You find prayer stultifying, because you are making it too elaborate and, for the humble, too difficult. You should avoid publicity and instead of thinking it important to pay God compliments, you should simply say 'Abba, Father'. There is no need to spend undue time, either, provided you concentrate on essentials.'

Christians are not so tempted these days to flaunt their devotion as once they may have been. It is more fashionable now to confess that you cannot pray, that the whole procedure is intellectually intolerable and wearisome in practice. Criticism and doubt are more likely to be heralded by trumpet blasts than are pious exercises. But there are those who have found prayer a burden because they have thought of it as the maintenance of a ceaseless barrage of words to bombard God into submission to their desires. To free ourselves from this, it is better to regard the Lord's Prayer as a series of very brief petitions, by which we may, as a Russian Orthodox counselled, stand before God with our mind in our heart. Prayer is not always and for everyone a verbal and mental process. It is the practice of withdrawal from the activities, responsibilities and cares of living, of quietly lifting up the restless and overburdened mind to God and leaving it there! Familiar words of trust may help us to do this, but they will be brief and we shall not bother about their exegesis. They will be but the stairway by which we gently climb into his presence.

This withdrawal is not escape. It may not be for long; it may not mean that we go to a special building. The 'secret place' of the Gospel may be the 'store room' (Matthew 6:6) or any place where we are doing our work and no one need be aware that our minds are with God. A few minutes of detachment may suffice and then we return, refreshed and strengthened to the Divine service on earth.

But there is more to the Lord's Prayer than this. We must consider its content, and when we do so, John Newton's words seem the best commentary:

> Thou art coming to a King;
> *Large* petitions with thee bring.

The prayer asks for nothing less than the Kingdom of God. In the very difficult, but profound epilogue to his book, *Secular Christianity*, Ronald Gregor Smith says that *Prayer is the anticipation in the whole of our existence of that one end which is the reality of God*. It seems to me that this also is the kind of definition which the Lord's Prayer demands. Prayer is not self-help or the Christian's secret of a happy life, or part of the therapy of personal integration. It is not an adjunct of living; it is life, directed towards God and his rule. In this sense, work is prayer and thought is prayer, eating is prayer and pleasure is prayer. We shall need time set aside for worship and contemplation—to question this is madness for most of us—but only that the whole of our existence may look towards the one end, which is the reality of God.

Every petition of the Lord's Prayer is about God and the Kingdom of God. The notoriously difficult crux is 'Give us this day our daily bread', in which the word translated 'daily' is rare and uncertain. 'Give us today tomorrow's bread' would seem to be more accurate, but 'tomorrow' for the Jew of the first century would mean the great tomorrow of the Kingdom of God. 'Give us today a fore-taste of the bread which we may eat with you in the King-dom' is probably the true meaning, and, of this, the 'Give us today the bread of life' of the second of *Modern Liturgical Texts* seems adequate shorthand for public repetition. The long-held belief that this clause has rele-vance to the Eucharist is entirely justified, for it is there, above all, that we look towards the one great end of our lives and the universe, and share by anticipation in the perfect life and love of heaven. 'Give us today, as we eat in the Sacrament, to know the joy of the feast in your kingdom.'

Similarly, 'Forgive us our sins, as we have forgiven those who wrong us', is best understood in the light of the belief in the coming of the Kingdom as the age of forgiveness. Professor Jeremias has paraphrased it like this:

O Lord, we indeed belong to the age of the Messiah, to the age of forgiveness, and we are ready to pass on to others the forgiveness which we receive. Now grant us, dear Father, the gift of the age of salvation, thy forgiveness. We stretch out our hands, forgive us our debts—even now, even here, already today.

An alternative paraphrase could be: 'Father, let our for-giveness of one another now be worthy of the forgiveness which we hope for from you, in your kingdom. Let this family of your people live by your forgiveness which we need so desperately.'

This indeed makes the Lord's Prayer terrible, for so many of us could not endure the Kingdom of God, and the anticipation of it, of 'that one end which is the reality of God' must be for us the vision of hell. To say the Lord's Prayer must be to travel the purgative way through fire and fierce temptation to the renewal of our mind.

In *Living Prayer*, Archbishop Anthony Bloom suggests that it is sometimes best to begin the Lord's Prayer from the end—'Deliver us from evil' and to see it as a journey like the Exodus of Israel from the Egypt of bondage, to the Promised Land of God's Kingdom. He works this out most pregnantly and shows how each petition corresponds to a different stage of that long and harassing pilgrimage until at last we come to Mount Zion and call God 'Our Father'. He is careful to point out that for Christians this is the beginning too; that anyone who approaches the Lord, in faith, may say 'Our Father', but once we start to grasp the meaning of the prayer we shall find that we have set out on a long road which we must follow in spite of its hazards else we shall die in the wilderness, or be driven back to the servitude of Egypt.

In another chapter of his book, Archbishop Anthony corrects the somewhat snobbish belief that petition is 'the lowest level' of prayer. In fact it presupposes much greater faith than praise or thanksgiving and no one should look askance at it. Perhaps there are those today who need to undertake a long journey of life and faith before they come to the point when they can honestly find a God who can be addressed and petitioned. More than one recent writer or speaker has suggested that for our time contemplation may be the beginning of prayer and not, as in the schemes of traditional mystic theology, the goal. That may, as far as this life goes, be *asking*.

In the eleventh chapter of St Luke's Gospel, written for Gentiles, for people who had not been brought up in the Jewish discipline of prayer, the *Our Father* is primarily a series of petitions. And the parable which accompanies it, teaches persistence in asking. It tells of a man, who was surprised by an unexpected visitor late at night when his larder was empty and he went to borrow bread from a neighbour. He was refused because of the inconvenience of the hour, but would not take 'No!' for an answer. He remained banging at the neighbour's door until, through sheer exasperation, he was given what he wanted.

Christians are to pray like this for the Kingdom of God, which includes the material order. But as we have said, some of those tinged with the scepticism of our modern philosophy may not be able to begin here. Perhaps they will only come to an understanding of the heavenly bread as they seek to provide earthly bread for the hungry. Péguy's dictum may have to be temporarily reversed and everything begin in politics and end in mysticism, not the other way round. Perhaps God wants to compel some Christians to talk to men, recognizing the full personality of all of them whatever their race or class, before he will give us the assurance of conversation with himself.

But the Lord's Prayer demands our third definition, that of H. H. Farmer: *Prayer is essentially the response of man's spirit to the ultimate as personal.* It is because this has not been taken with full seriousness that some people have found the words 'lead us not into temptation' so difficult and have resorted to such futile devices as suggesting a comma after 'lead us', which does nothing at all to change the sense but seems to satisfy the puzzled, perhaps because it shows a resolution for change. There is understandable resistance to the idea that God would 'ensnare our will into evil choices', but if the prayer is thought of as conversation with a Father, there is no real problem at all. A little child about to cross a main road with his Father could well cry as he clutched his parent's hand amid the traffic's fury, 'Daddy, don't let me get run over'.* Similarly, we pray 'lead us not into temptation; when the great tests come, do not let us fall'. It is the old prayer, 'Save us!', and only a perilous self-confidence will make us feel that it is not necessary and perhaps more so when we seem most secure against the obvious trials.

---

* I owe this illustration to the Reverend A. Raymond George.

The intellectual difficulty which so many of our contemporaries feel about the personality of the ultimate is one which must prove the steel of Christian philosophers. We had to refer to this in Chapter Two and all that is necessary to add here is that the full meaning of Christian prayer is not discovered until, as one of the preliminary draft documents for the Uppsala Assembly put it, 'the creature addresses the reality of its Creator as "Thou" '. This is not to say that the Church must lose sympathy for those who cannot honestly do this or deny them its membership. But it is one of the tasks of the Church in this 'secular' age to help men to understand prayer as communion with a personal God, for this, apart from everything else, is the only way to save humanity. The Uppsala draft goes on:

Prayer is the creative struggle of a love that cannot and would not wish to escape the pattern of Gethsemane and the Cross. It is no easy matter to discover and respond to the world as a place so fashioned that, within a context of personal relationships, human persons are emerging in it; but this is the challenge of joy and the enticement of love.

We said at the opening of this chapter, echoing St Paul, that it is only in the Holy Spirit that we can pray the Lord's Prayer, only, that is, in the community of those who are in the relationship to God which Christ has made possible for us, who live by the life of God, which his death released, and who are ready to watch with him in Gethsemane and, if need be, take up the Cross which he appoints.

The privilege and the responsibility of saying the Lord's Prayer is ours because of what Christ has done. We may call God Father because he cried out 'My God, my God, why hast thou forsaken me?' We may work and suffer for the Kingdom of God, because, in dying, he opened it to all believers.

Jesus taught the Lord's Prayer, not only in the Sermon

on the Mount, but from the Cross on the Hill. No wonder when it occurs in the worship, which brings us to his passion and victory, it is introduced in words which affirm our humble confidence:

And now, as our Lord hath taught us, we are bold to say, Our Father. . . .

For Recollection

Abba, Father . . . thy will be done.

God, help us to watch with Christ in Gethsemane and not to sleep through fear or sloth, indifference to thy love or the desire to evade our responsibilities. . . . In the garden Christ asked in faith and accepted in faith. He wrestled with his lot and rebelled against what men would do to him and then yielded as to the loving purpose of a dear Father.

Lord, my will is mine.

I am the prisoner of circumstances I did not wholly
    contrive,
in a world I did not make,
with a temperament I inherited;
Yet, Lord, my will is mine.

I am influenced by other people,
by the latest fashions of dress and thought and speech,
often dominated by powers I cannot control;
Yet, Lord, my will is mine.

I did not choose to be born or decide the hour,
I do not know what the future holds
for myself or those I love,
the time and manner of my death are hidden from me;
Yet, Lord, my will is mine *now*:
MY WILL IS MINE TO MAKE IT YOURS.

77

SEVEN

The Prayer of Humble Access

We do not presume to come to this Thy Table, O merciful Lord, trusting in our own righteousness, but in Thy manifold and great mercies. We are not worthy so much as to gather up the crumbs under Thy Table. But Thou art the same Lord, whose property is always to have mercy: Grant us therefore, gracious Lord, so to eat the flesh of Thy dear Son Jesus Christ, and to drink His blood, that our sinful bodies may be made clean by His body, and our souls washed through His most precious blood, and that we may evermore dwell in Him, and He in us. *Amen*
(*The Book of Common Prayer*)

Lord we come to your table trusting in your mercy and not in any goodness of our own.
We are not worthy even to gather up the crumbs under your table,
but it is your nature always to have mercy,
and on that we depend.
Grant that we may so eat the flesh of Jesus Christ your Son and drink his blood,
that we may for ever live in him and he in us. *Amen*
(*The Sunday Service*,
Methodist Conference, 1968)

THIS prayer, which the Scottish Prayer Book of 1637, calls the *Collect* of Humble Access to the Holy Communion, was composed by Archbishop Thomas Cranmer, sometime in the 1540s. The late Dom Gregory Dix once decided, in conversation with a friend, that it must have been written on a summer's afternoon of poetic inspiration, and, like all such works, has been something of an embarrassment ever since!

In spite of his incalculable services to English Christianity, Thomas Cranmer is more criticized than admired.

Like St Paul, it is not his fate to be popular! In *A Man for All Seasons,* he appears as a feeble time-server, in contrast to the conscientious and Catholic Chancellor. Yet he was far less intolerant of his opponents than the now sainted More. He was, perhaps, a diplomatist. There is ambiguity about his recantation of the Protestant faith under Queen Mary, and, at the end, his recantation of his recantation! But no close student of his life and times will find him lacking in courage.

Anglo-Catholics have tended not to like Cranmer because he was a Protestant and became increasingly so as he went on. Traditional Methodists have a love-hate relation to the *Book of Common Prayer* but do not feel particular regard or honour for its compiler. The *avant garde* do not approve of his theology or of his Order of Communion. His language seems archaic and too resplendent and his liturgy is over-weighted with penitence, too concentrated on the Cross. It has even been called 'one long Good Friday'. Much of the antipathy from all sides is concentrated upon this prayer. I want to take what may seem to be the somewhat unusual course of expounding it by examining four objections.

(1) Its position in the Communion Service of 1552-1662, the Anglican and Methodist order, is deemed unfortunate. In Cranmer's first Prayer Book of 1549, it was placed after the Prayer of Consecration, and before the distribution of bread and wine, a position to which it may return in any revision of the Anglican Series II, and which it has, optionally, in the new Methodist Service. But in the Prayer Book it comes after *Lift up your hearts* and the *Holy, holy, holy* before the prayer which recalls the action of Jesus in the Upper Room. This is said, in the technical language of liturgiologists, to 'mutilate the canon', to interrupt the great thanksgiving, to bring us back to penitence just when we should be celebrating the victory of Christ.

But if you forget the other liturgies of Christendom and

take Cranmer's service on its merits, you will see that it has a powerful and dramatic effect all its own. We lift up our hearts and praise God with 'angels and archangels and all the company of heaven'. For a while, the veil is rent and we are there in the eternal order with the redeemed in the glory of God. And then, suddenly, even before the echoes of the angels' song have died away, we remember that we are, after all, totally undeserving of this high worship and entirely out of place in such company. 'We do not presume . . .'. Only because of what Christ has done for us are we able even to glimpse such glories. And so, after the rapture of praise, we come humbly to the Saviour's board. Like Charles Simeon, the Cambridge evangelical, we are sinners, though forgiven sinners, to the last. And perhaps our joy is greater than that of the angelic hosts, when we, in the knowledge of our unworthiness, are yet bidden by the Lord himself to be his guests.

(2) A more academic criticism to which I must refer, briefly, concerns the prayer that 'our sinful bodies may be made clean by his body and our souls washed through his most precious blood'. This involves a curious dichotomy, which is found in St Thomas Aquinas and earlier. There is, indeed, a Syriac form of the Liturgy of St James, which would not be known to Cranmer, which has this petition—'Vouchsafe us, O Lord God, that our bodies may be made holy by Thy holy Body, and our souls made radiant by the propitiatory Blood'.

Behind this lies Leviticus 17:11—'The life of the flesh is in the blood'. It could lead to an excessively high value being placed upon the chalice and to this being restricted to the priests. Yet the Protestant Reformers interpreted it in the opposite way to justify communion in both kinds, and perhaps this is why Cranmer used these words—to assert that the whole Christ, in the whole Sacrament is for all believers.

Nowadays it is not necessary to use this defence of the cup being given to the people. And so the recent revisions say, as does Series II, which the Methodists have copied, 'Grant us therefore, gracious Lord, so to eat the flesh of thy dear Son Jesus Christ, and to drink his blood, that we may evermore dwell in him and he in us'.

(3) Is not the prayer too grovelling? Is 'humble access' altogether Christian? A lady was once seated next to a recently appointed Cardinal at a dinner party. She decided to ask a leading question. 'I expect, your Eminence, that when you knew you were going to be made Cardinal, you prayed for humility?' 'No, madam,' he replied, 'for confidence'.

Is not that what we really need? The humanists and the psychologists would tell us that man must enter into his kingdom and claim it boldly. In his book *On NOT leaving it to the Snake* Harvey Cox gives a novel interpretation of the story of Adam and Eve, in which he suggests that Eve's sin was not pride. It was letting a serpent tell her what to do. If that be thought over-ingenious, there is no doubt that Adam's misery lay in the fear which made him hide instead of facing God, while the wretched man who buried his talent in the ground, certainly, suffered from lack of confidence. He appears cautious, conformist, refusing to take risks. He did not 'presume'. The woman in the story which is recalled in the words about gathering the crumbs from under the table, did not say to Jesus when he refused at first to heal her daughter, 'We are not worthy'. She made a bold retort 'Even the dogs gather up the children's crumbs!' This showed her faith and brought healing. She did not cringe in guilty fear, but advanced boldly to take her share of God's bounty, outsider as she was.

The worst criminals of our time, apart from satanic figures such as Hitler, have been servile 'yes-men', who would not assert themselves against tyrants, but accepted the evil around them because they were too timid to demand justice. They would not oppose authority.

This lack of confidence is often apparent with regard to Holy Communion. People say 'I am not worthy' as an excuse for absence from the Table of the Lord. They claim that the mystery is too wonderful for them and that they are afraid of eating and drinking damnation.

There is a long history of this reluctance and most great Christian teachers, such as the Puritans and John Wesley, have had to deal with it. Sometimes it is the excuse of sheer sloth. At best it misunderstands the Gospel of him who came not to call the righteous but sinners to repentance and opened his feast to all and sundry from the streets. It can be inverted pride, as John Cassian knew when he attacked those monks who, in order to be thoroughly prepared, come to communion but once a year:

They run the risk of greater arrogance than they fancy themselves to avoid, because when they do receive, they judge themselves worthy to receive. To partake every Sunday to heal our sickness, in the humility of heart which confesses that we can never worthily approach these holy mysteries, is far better than in pride to believe at the end of a year that we are worthy to receive.

This strikes the balance. We must come to the Lord's Table, we must live our Christian lives in confidence, but in *humble* confidence. It is necessary that in our world man should not shirk his mastery of things and that he should assume his political and social responsibilities. Many of the ills of mankind could be overcome if people did not evade the confrontation with evil, if they realized their power and did not allow the forces of government or big business or the world banks to dictate their lives and apportion wealth and maintain their spheres of influence by terror.

This is the lesson that student power is trying to teach us and no Christian should merely scorn or deride or dismiss it as young-thuggery. And yet arrogance is a very horrid thing and we know what Lord Acton said about power—that it tends to corrupt and absolute power corrupts absolutely. There is in our time a danger that megalomania, formerly the disease of leaders and tyrants, will become democratized, that it will be caught by those who have hitherto been, perhaps unreasonably, repressed, especially the young; that they will feel that wisdom began with them and forget that because their fathers have eaten sour grapes—of which they are well aware—their own teeth are set on edge. In the end megalomania leads to nihilism. Lacking in reverence for God or man, for the past, the present or the future, eager only to assert power, its victims pull down the whole edifice of human life.

We should not be too proud to admit that we derive all our joy and sustenance from God, who is not the supreme megalomaniac, but the suffering God, who invites us to his table and waits on us himself, whose bounty is his very life, his flesh and blood given for his world. Therefore 'we do not presume . . .'. *But we come!*

(4) And yet just here is the biggest objection of all to the prayer. 'To eat the flesh of thy dear Son Jesus Christ and to drink his blood.' This is surely the crudest and most carnal paganism and many refined and Christian spirits are revolted by it. An eminent man of letters known to me confessed that he was repelled by the retention of this prayer in the new Methodist rite. And he is not alone. On a majority vote the prayer would not survive. Yet the quarrel is not with Cranmer but with St John. It is ironic that my literary friend finds John supreme among the Gospels and would make the discourses from the Upper Room his viaticum. Yet in the sixth chapter the author of the most spiritual of all the Gospels can write 'Except ye eat the flesh of the Son of man and drink his blood, ye have not life in yourselves'. Why should this be so?

First, and principally, because St John must stress the

83

reality of our union with Christ. There is something almost physical in its closeness. He becomes as much a part of us as our food.

Second, to bring home to us the brute reality of Christ's death on the Cross. He conquered not by edifying words or a noble philosophy taught in academic groves, but by blood, toil, tears, and sweat. His was not the appearance of suffering, but the reality.

And this is what being a Christian may mean: an awful unity with Christ even in his Passion. 'Except ye eat the flesh of the Son of man, and drink his blood, ye have no life in you.' We are to receive a Crucified Saviour.

We must not, above all, in Holy Communion, brood morbidly, masochistically upon the dreadful tortures of the Cross. But we must understand that the world is not saved by good advice from an ivory tower or even by the more satisfying tasks of human compassion, in which I would include not only some of the more glamorous philanthropic adventures, but the occasional fast and the generous donation. The world is saved as we enter the arena of conflict, which may mean politics and war, and being racked and torn if need be in the process.

There is, of course, joy in the Gospel, celebration in the Eucharist and pleasure in life. Much of our time, please God, we shall thoroughly enjoy ourselves and sample to the full the delights of the Church and the world. Even the martyrs died not many times before their deaths. And Jesus was not perpetually the Man of Sorrows, while now he reigns in glory. But we eat his flesh and drink his blood to show our oneness with him in all that he does, or seeks to do again, in our flesh, for the life of the world.

Thank God for the realism of this language. It happens to be the very nerve of our faith. We must not be squeamish. We must understand what it means, not to stand beneath the Cross or to shelter behind it, but to share it and know well what it is to eat and drink with Christ.

We will not deceive ourselves into imagining that to go to the Lord's Supper is to be crucified with Christ or that this outward act is the limit of our discipleship. But, at times, especially in Lent, it is good that our celebration should be solemn, that we should for once reflect on the seriousness of being a Christian, on the gravity of the Gospel.

Christ went to the Cross; do not let us always be content to 'trip along' to happy family worship or even to communion. God's commitment to the human race meant the flies and stench and racking pain of Calvary. His mercy is not as the gentle rain from heaven but as the blood of a crucified man dripping to the ground. And we, who are always in search of some ideology or grand intellectual scheme to end our troubles, are bidden leave our contemplations and find the hope of the world and our own immortality in the wounds of Jesus and in the fellowship of his sufferings, as we kneel to receive the bread and wine.

He which hath said of the one sacrament wash and be clean, hath said concerning the other likewise, eat and live . . . these misteries doe as nails fasten us to his verie Crosse, that by them we draw out, as touching efficacie force and vertue, euen the blood of his goared side. . . .'*

---

* Richard Hooker, *Of the Laws of Ecclesiastical Politie*, v.67.

A Twentieth-century Act of
Preparation for Holy Communion

How shall I come?

As I am—I could not come otherwise—with my muddled ideas on the meaning of life and my complex personality, so immersed in getting and spending and the relationships of every day, so *earthy* in my desires and temptations and yet with a strange hunger and thirst for the life I think I see in Christ and the saints, for ultimate reality as against the passing show and subterfuge of the dimension in which I spend much of my time.

I shall come seeking . . . even though I do not know precisely what . . . .

I shall come, too, out of loyalty to my fellow Christians throughout the world, who 'do this' because they believe Christ told them to.

I shall try to prepare my mind just a little, if possible by reading the Order of Service beforehand with the Scripture passages to be used that day.

If nothing else, I shall say a prayer rather like this:

Lord, help me to join with your people on earth and in heaven to celebrate your love and be one with you in your continuing purpose for all men and all creation.

But I must also decide who I am going to take with me. Members of my family may be coming too, but I ought to join in Christian worship with a specific intention directed as a rule to someone other than myself, who may not be present—friends who are getting married, young people starting out in life, the nations of the world, the hungry, the sick.

We would not come alone, dear Lord,
To Thy great feast, and at Thy board
  In rapture sit and gaze;
But bring the lost, the sick, the lone,
The little ones to be Thine own,
  And look into Thy face.

'What will he say to us if we go to him without the others?'

What happens when I am there?

There may be felt inspiration, a powerful sermon, fine music and a sense of Christ's presence.

It may be all anti-climax, badly organized, the microphone out of order, the preacher not at his best, a dull and wearisome formality and I shall be like stone as I receive the bread and wine.

My thoughts may wander, to the golf course, or the man or woman I love, or to some wretched problem of my life and work, and the service will seem antiquarian and irrelevant and have nothing to say to me at all.

Perhaps there is something wrong with me and I need to go to the root of my being and talk over my failure to respond with the Minister or a friend.

But I ought to fasten on to something—some phrase in prayer, Scripture or sermon, some action or demand. If the heavenly thoughts won't come I ought to ask how the love which the service is supposed to proclaim—even though it is done so badly—may reach others through me?

And there's always that 'intention'. What ought I to do for So-and-so, or as my contribution to world peace, or freedom from hunger?

Sometimes I shall want to still my mind altogether, not even listen to the sermon, and rest in the movement of worship from preparation to final blessing and try to relax completely, carried along by the drama of the liturgy. In all this, whether I am conscious of him or no, Christ will be uniting me in the fellowship of his people with the progress of his love from first creation to the end of the world.

And I must never forget that I am a member of the congregation. I must not simply regard the service as the background to my own private thoughts.

I must join in hymns, responses, prayers as best I can and remember that if I do not feel Christ's presence at his Table, it may be because he wants me to see him in my neighbour in church, whether familiar or a stranger, congenial or distasteful, friend or opponent.

What should happen afterwards?

I shall probably get caught up in friendly words with the dispersing people before I become immersed once again in the cares or pleasures of my own particular relationships. Sometimes I shall need to go away quietly by myself and think over again what has happened and what its demand on me is. But this may not often be allowed me.

The Service ought to come back to me during the week and the opportunity for its application will be not in 'devotions' but in duty, as I make my domestic or business decisions and deal with the people I meet.

It is good if I may take hymns and lessons and read them again in the course of the days or discuss them with family or friends, but most important of all is *action*. '*DO* this in remembrance of me.' I myself with my fellow Christians must become the sacrament of God's love to the world. Christ says, not only of the eucharistic bread but of the Church: THIS IS MY BODY.

> *O God, who hast prepared for them that love thee*
> *such good things as pass man's understanding:*
> *Pour into our hearts such love toward thee, that*
> *we, loving thee above all things, may obtain thy*
> *promises, which exceed all that we can desire;*
> *through Jesus Christ our Lord.* Amen
> BOOK OF COMMON PRAYER